Understanding Grammar in Scotland Today

John Corbett
Christian Kay

THE ASSOCIATION FOR SCOTTISH LITERARY STUDIES
Glasgow 2009

Published in Great Britain, 2009
by The Association for Scottish Literary Studies
Department of Scottish Literature
University of Glasgow
7 University Gardens
Glasgow G12 8QH

www.asls.org.uk

ISBN: 978-0-948877-93-3

A catalogue record for this book
is available from the British Library.

The Association for Scottish Literary Studies acknowledges
support from the Scottish Arts Council towards
the publication of this book.

Printed and bound by Bell & Bain Ltd, Glasgow

Contents

Acknowledgements

This book is intended to introduce undergraduates, teachers and senior school pupils to the formal study of grammar. An innovative feature of the book is that it draws its evidence from contemporary Scottish writing and speech, as they are found in the Scottish Corpus of Texts and Speech (SCOTS) – www.scottishcorpus.ac.uk. The book therefore serves as an introduction to the study of English as it is written and spoken in Scotland today, with some comments on Broad Scots, literary and colloquial. The SCOTS project benefited from a Resource Enhancement Grant awarded by the Arts and Humanities Research Council (www.ahrc.uk). Fellow project members, particularly Jean Anderson, Wendy Anderson and Dave Beavan, were generous in giving suggestions that have improved the volume.

Earlier versions of this book have been used over many years with first and second-year undergraduates at Glasgow University. The book is the basis for a course that involves approximately 15 contact hours of lectures and small-group workshops, but it can also be used as a reference book and for self-study. We are grateful to our colleagues and students in the Department of English Language who have used the book, commented on its strengths and weaknesses, and so helped us to refine it. From the perspective of experienced school teachers, Lorna Smith and Ronald Renton of the Education Committee of the ASLS provided welcome encouragement and valuable advice that shaped the present version of the book. Flora Edmonds and Duncan Jones lent their expertise to the production of the volume. The faults that remain are, needless to say, our own responsibility.

Chapter 1   Understanding Grammar

This Chapter outlines the general aims of this book, in particular introducing the concepts of *prescriptive* and *descriptive* grammar in the context of language use in Scotland. Language use in Scotland is characterised by a range of languages and language varieties, including different kinds of spoken Broad Scots and a fairly uniform standard variety of spoken and written English. Since our exploration of grammar in Scotland draws on an electronic archive of Scottish texts that encompass a range of language varieties, we need to explain whether this book is intended to inform its readers about what *should* be said and written (i.e. prescriptivism), or if it is intended to demonstrate what *is* said and written (i.e. descriptivism). A discussion of prescriptivism versus descriptivism is a necessary preamble to any description of grammatical features that draws upon evidence of the speech and writing of particular communities.

1.0   About this Book

This book has several aims:

- To introduce you to language investigation using the Scottish Corpus of Texts and Speech (the SCOTS corpus: www.scottishcorpus.ac.uk), a freely-available online web resource.
- To raise your skills and confidence in the analysis of sentences as they are written – and also spoken – in Scotland today. Chapters 1-8 of this book cover what is traditionally called 'parsing'. Parsing involves looking closely at a sentence or utterance, identifying the parts that make it up (i.e. its constituents) and considering how these constituents are related to each other in words, phrases, clauses and sentences.
- To give you a simple framework with which to think about the relationship between meaning and grammatical form, particularly in relation to the verb phrase (Chapters 9-12). As we shall see, the verb phrase is a key element in any well-structured sentence, and the many forms of the verb phrase express a multitude of subtle meanings.

- Chapter 13 looks at the application of the grammatical knowledge acquired in this book to past SQA 'Higher' English examinations, particularly questions that demand the close reading of unseen texts.

It is the first of the above aims that gives this grammar book its particular flavour. Advances in computing technology began to make a considerable impact on language studies in the early 1980s. For the first time, we can base our descriptions of language on large-scale collections of 'real' data that can be searched quickly and easily. Before the 1980s, descriptions of any language were based largely on the intuitions of the analyst – sometimes, but not always, supported by a relatively modest collection of usually written data that had been slowly assembled manually and painstakingly classified. Centuries of intuition combined with the analysis of mainly written documents afforded a rich set of theories and descriptions of language – but they were nonetheless limited in nature. Current descriptions of language combine the virtues of personal intuition about language behaviour with the availability of a powerful evidence base that tells us an immense amount about what people actually do – not just what we *think* they do.

The Scottish Corpus of Texts and Speech is one of a new generation of electronic archives. It is significant in size, at around four million words, and easily searchable for examples of linguistic features. As its name suggests, it contains spoken language as well as written, and so it offers the possibility of more comprehensive descriptions of language activity in Scotland than have hitherto been attempted. The SCOTS corpus includes many types of written and spoken text, from Scottish parliamentary proceedings to excerpts from contemporary fiction, and from everyday conversation to university lectures. The texts date from 1945 to the present day.

The main aim of this book is not, however, to present a comprehensive grammar of language as it is used in Scotland. That would take a book several times the length and complexity of this one! Its more modest aim is to give a brief guide to (i) how you can begin to develop the descriptive skills necessary to understand the nature of the written and spoken language you encounter in Scotland today, and (ii) how you can access the SCOTS corpus to develop that knowledge. That is to say, this basic introduction to grammatical analysis is *informed* by the SCOTS corpus. Many of the examples analysed in this book are taken from its electronic archive of written and spoken texts. These examples are shown in **bold type**. Of course, by removing them from their fuller context, some of these examples might occasionally seem strange. If you want to find out more about their original setting and see how they work in context, simply go to the SCOTS home page and type any given example into the *Quick Search* box.

Further information about searching the SCOTS corpus is given later in this Chapter.

A few words need to be said about what we mean by 'language use in Scotland' since the situation is fascinating, complex, and frequently misunderstood. Speech and writing in Scotland today is the result of a long and complicated history. Broadly speaking, we can argue that part of that history involves *contact* between two distinct language varieties – Broad Scots and standard Southern English – a contact that eventually created a third variety: Scottish English. Language users in Scotland can make use of any of these three varieties – Broad Scots, standard Southern English, Scottish English – in their speech and writing. This linguistic flexibility can lead to various outcomes, for example:

- Many people speak Broad Scots (at least in some situations) but use a standard written variety that is in most instances indistinguishable from Southern English, or indeed English written elsewhere.
- A smaller number choose to write in Broad Scots, often in poetry, fiction or drama.

- Some speak or write a variety that inclines towards Southern English but retains some traces of the Broad Scots system – this is what we would call Scottish English.

In truth, of course, this summary simplifies the complexity of the speech situation in Scotland, which includes contact among these three varieties and also other languages, in particular Scottish Gaelic and 'community languages' such as Urdu, Chinese and Polish, which have arrived with more recent immigration and settlement. In addition, the mass media expose language users in Scotland to many other varieties of global English, such as American and Australian English, as well as other varieties of English from the British Isles. And we must not forget that language contact and variety is not confined to spoken and written language – the Deaf Community in Scotland has different varieties of British Sign Language, a visual code that is influenced by communicative practices locally, and further afield. And all these languages and language varieties are continually changing, in part as a consequence of mutual exposure.

Clearly, not even the 4 million words of the SCOTS corpus can capture all this complexity, but focusing our attention on authentic data from contemporary Scottish speech and writing has the virtue of locating us in the realm of what is actually said and written in the country today.

1.1   What do we Mean by 'Grammar'?

The word 'grammar' is one of the most loaded terms in the language. It also means different things to different people. The word is most commonly understood to refer to the way language is used in general. Many people feel strongly that there is a right way of using language, and a wrong way. The 'right' way of using language is considered 'grammatical' and the 'wrong' way is considered 'ungrammatical'. According to this view, learning 'grammar' means learning how to use language 'properly'.

Let us consider this view for a moment. Look at the following sentences and ask yourself which you would consider to be grammatically incorrect. (As noted above, examples taken from the SCOTS corpus are given in **bold** type. The example sentences in each chapter are numbered.) Then, ask yourself *why* you have come to this decision:

1. **Parliamentary Committees will be required to formally declare any interests which they may have.**
2. **I seen there was a message on your phone.**
3. **'I do wish you'd find another crowd to run with.'**
4. This the something scrambled words all seems have to in sentence.

4

Most people would argue that (2) and (4) are grammatically incorrect, but if you think about it, they are 'incorrect' for different reasons.

First of all, sentence (4) simply does not make sense; in order to be understood, the words would have to be rearranged, to make something like *Something seems to have scrambled all the words in this sentence*. This tells us something fundamental about grammar – namely, that the order of words is important for our understanding. To make sense, words have to be arranged according to certain rules, which in turn suggests that they relate to each other in specific ways. For example, a word like 'the' has to precede a word like 'words' rather than a word like 'seems'. Sentence (4) does not follow these rules, and so it is ungrammatical.

Example (2), however, *does* make sense. The issue here is with the expression 'I seen'. This expression is comprehensible, and indeed, especially in cities like Glasgow, Belfast and, in this case, Aberdeen, many people say things like 'I seen', 'He's went', 'She's ran away' and 'I've swam'. There are over twenty examples of *I seen* recorded in the SCOTS corpus. However, fewer people would write these phrases, and a glance at the corpus examples shows that the only written examples are indeed in literary texts that seek to represent spoken forms. The reason for this distinction between the conventions of speech and the conventions of writing is that there are different dialects or varieties of English. One of these dialects is associated with the written word, which itself influences 'educated' speech: this dialect is usually referred to as 'standard English'. According to the conventions of standard English, *I seen* is unacceptable, and the 'correct' form should be *I saw*. Sentence (2) is ungrammatical, then, if your point of reference is this educated, mainly written, variety of English.

However, as is evident from the SCOTS corpus, many people *say* things like *I seen* and even if their usage is frowned upon by some others, they still manage to be understood. If a language variety can be understood, then it too must, like standard English, be governed by rules and conventions that allow its speakers to make sense of it. In this technical sense, non-standard varieties of English and all the dialects of Scots *are* grammatical, and their grammars can be described. In short, we can say that forms like *I seen* are ungrammatical with respect to the written dialect of standard English, but they are grammatical with respect to the everyday usage of many Scottish speakers.

Sentences (1) and (3) are possibly more controversial. Many people would regard them as grammatical, even in terms of standard English, and pass them by without further comment. A few, however, might pause and argue that both are in fact ungrammatical. Why should this be so?

Sentence (1) contains an example of 'a split infinitive'. The problem here, for some, is that the phrase 'to declare' (the infinitive) has been 'split' by the word 'formally'. Traditionally, teachers of standard English grammar used to argue that the infinitive – expressions like 'to go', 'to swim', 'to speak', and so on – should not be split, or separated, by the insertion of other words like 'boldly', 'quickly' or 'loudly'. The expression, '*to* boldly *go*', beloved of *Star Trek* fans, is therefore grammatically incorrect – if you believe traditionalists.

The problem with Sentence (3) is that it ends with the word 'with'. (This example is taken from Sheena Blackhall's short story, 'The Fower Quarters 02: Purity'.) 'With' is a member of a class of little words called *prepositions*. Traditionalists might argue that grammatical sentences should never end with prepositions. You can possibly place the preposition earlier in the sentence, revising it as 'I do wish you'd find another crowd with which to run'. That little change might keep the traditionalist happy, though it might in fact lead to an awkward, stiffer, more formal-sounding sentence that few people would actually say aloud or write.

However, most people would probably feel that the rules that make Sentences (1) and (3) seem ungrammatical to the traditionalist are unjustified. Eloquent speakers and writers of standard English have been splitting infinitives and ending sentences with prepositions for centuries. Where are the traditionalists getting their rules from, then? The answer is that the 'tradition' which they are relying on is only about 250 years old. During the eighteenth century, teachers started writing down the rules of standard English grammar for use in schools. They had no readily-available models for doing this, so they went to what they knew best: the rules of Latin, then the most respected language in Europe, and the language most closely associated with education since the Middle Ages.

English grammarians, then, assumed that all other languages should follow the model of Latin. In Latin grammar, the infinitive is not made up of two words; it is only one word, such as *amare* ('to love'). Since you cannot normally split a single word, the rule about not splitting infinitives was born. Similarly, no Latin writer could end a sentence with a preposition – Latin simply doesn't work like that – so that rule was also transferred to English schoolbooks by eighteenth-century grammarians and teachers. Few teachers and grammarians today would apply the rules of one language to another – however, certain traditionalists continue to apply the criteria devised by eighteenth-century language experts to present-day speech behaviour. There is no doubt that there is some satisfaction in attending to and following traditional rules of language behaviour that mark one out as a member of an educated elite; equally, by refusing to follow such rules, speakers and writers can signal their resistance to what may be regarded as elitism. Grammatical usage, and the teaching of grammar, have thus been drawn into the class war.

By now it will be clear that the terms 'grammatical' and 'ungrammatical' are used in different ways:

(i)   to refer to the way words are put together to make sense;
(ii)   to refer to the conventions governing a standard dialect only;
(iii) to refer to a traditional set of rules of language behaviour, formulated in the eighteenth century, and used today, by some, as the basis of a kind of linguistic etiquette.

This book is concerned with the first of these points. It introduces you to basic grammatical concepts and trains you in a method of grammatical analysis that is systematic and suitable for complete beginners. The book assumes that you have had no previous experience of studying English grammar formally. However, as well as giving you a basic grounding in grammatical terms and methods of analysis, this book will prepare you to study grammatical theory further, if you wish to do so. If you have studied some grammar before, some of the procedures used here may seem unusual; however, many will be familiar and should only require a little adaptation from the descriptive procedures you already know.

1.2   Descriptive and Prescriptive Grammars

In focusing on the first of the three meanings of 'grammar' noted above, we shall be attempting to devise a framework of concepts and 'rules' that allow us to analyse sentences and utterances that make sense. The concepts and 'rules' of our grammar describe what people *actually* do in order to be understood, not what they *should* do in order to be socially acceptable, though we touch on that topic in passing here and there. Because our main goal will be description, we can call our model of language behaviour a *descriptive grammar*. This name distinguishes our grammar from a set of rules which must be followed if a person wishes to be thought of as 'educated'.   Such a set of regulations is usually called a *prescriptive grammar*.

At first glance, a descriptive grammar might seem much less useful than a prescriptive grammar. Many people, for example learners of English as a First, Second or Other Language, might reasonably wish to use a prescriptive grammar to help them gain access to the prestigious standard variety of

English. Many teachers, pupils and students actively demand firm guidance on what is grammatically 'correct' and what is not. So why would anyone simply wish to describe what people do 'naturally'? There are a number of possible answers to this question. Most of them assume that there is more to language than a written, standard variety.

Describing Language Varieties

First of all, it is useful for the student or teacher of English to have even a basic understanding of the processes involved in describing and accounting for actual language behaviour. Anyone who is studying language as it is used in everyday life will come across expressions like:

5. Give it him.
6. **Give it to him.**
7. **Ye didnae have wardrobes or presses in them days.**
8. **It was a smaller town in those days.**

The *prescriptive* grammarian would simply ask which of the above conforms to the conventions of standard English. The prescriptive grammarian would therefore argue that (6) and (8) – and possibly (5), which is common in British English but not found in the SCOTS corpus – are correct and acceptable. Example (7) breaks several rules from the perspective of standard English: it has a non-standard negative particle, *-nae,* and it uses *them* rather than *those* to identify *days.* A *descriptive* grammarian, on the other hand, would assume that all four examples are equally grammatical, and he or she would investigate the different rules governing each. He or she might then go on to ask which groups of people systematically use these rules and when. The descriptivist explorer of language may then come to a deeper understanding of how language varies according to speech community and situation.

English and Scots are often thought of as being on a *language continuum.* This means that they are mutually intelligible varieties of language, and there is no absolute point where one shades into the other. Much of the SCOTS corpus contains, at one end of the continuum, many texts in written standard English, as in this excerpt from Scottish Parliamentary records:

9. **Organised crime continues to flood our streets with drugs, challenging the ability of our police to keep order. Any regulation of investigatory powers must therefore put the right of the individual and society to be free from fear of intimidation and drugs before the rights of any individual involved in illegally disrupting lives through the pursuit of organised criminal activity.**

At the other end of the continuum, there are texts in the SCOTS corpus in a dense, localised Broad Scots. The following short story, 'Dirty Beasts' by Alexander Fenton, from the collection *Craiters,* contains many Scots forms that imitate speech (e.g. in the spellings of *cd* for *could* and *mn* for *maun* 'must'):

10. **Ere wis a lot o history in at wid, an in e palins roon aboot it. Ye niver jist kent fit new thing ye mith come upon. Een o ma ploys fin I wis a loon wis tae set weer snares – e great hunter, ye ken – fae e nethmist straans o e palins faar I cd see e rabbits' runs. Weel, we'd a cat eence aboot e craft, a great big strippit beast caad Timoshenko. It wis ill for wannerin miles oot aboot, seein till its ain gamekeepin. Ae time it wis tint for days, till it managet tae get craalt hame wi a snare roon its neck. It likely used up mair'n some o its lifes on at expedeetion, an it mn a been lyin somewye tit-tittin at e weer for days an nichts or it knackit e straans, een be een, an won lowse.**

Excerpts (9) and (10) are situated at extreme ends of the standard English-Broad Scots language continuum. In between, where most speech and writing occurs, we find texts in the hybrid Scottish English, often shifting backwards and forwards between the two poles, as in example (11), an excerpt from a family letter by Madge Law, which, although it is written largely in standard English, shifts towards broader Scots in the final paragraph:

11. **Remember what I told you don't bring any towels or lots of luggage I've got plenty of towels and your clothes can all be washed and dried here. I've been to the supermarket and bought plenty of flour, I thought you might fancy making some cakes here if the weather is wet. The weather hasn't been very good through June until now so lets hope its a bit nicer by the time you get here.**

    Well I'll say ta ta for noo and we will have a good blether when you both come.

Since many language users in Scotland shift between English and Scots when speaking and writing, the designers of the SCOTS corpus have not labelled their documents as being in one or the other language variety. The methods of grammatical analysis described in this book apply equally to both varieties of language.

Comparing Languages

Some teachers and students of language might be interested in comparing the rules of English to those governing other languages, such as French, Polish, Chinese or Arabic. As noted above in relation to eighteenth-century grammarians and Latin, you cannot simply apply the rules of one language to another. The way different languages put words together to express meaning can be quite different, and often revealing of the mind-set of another culture. For example, consider *why* in English the following expressions are considered acceptable or unacceptable (throughout this book, an asterisk (*) indicates an unacceptable word, phrase or sentence). Then think about how you would explain to an overseas learner of English when to use the word *much* and when to use the word *many*.

12. **they widnae be tempted tae eat *too much rabbit***
13. **a mind heated with *too much study* of romantic English literature**
14. *…they widnae be tempted tae eat *too many rabbit*
15. *…a mind heated with *too many study* of romantic English literature
16. **There are far *too many private conversations* going on…**
17. **It emerged that *too many youngsters* were failing…**
18. *There are far *too much private conversations* going on…
19. *It emerged that *too much youngsters* were failing…

The answer is that there is a grammatical rule in English governing the use of *much* and *many*:

- *many* is used to quantify items that can be counted, like youngsters, or conversations.
- *much* is used to quantify items that are uncountable because they are generally conceptualised as abstract masses. Here, 'study' is clearly an abstract concept, and even, in context, 'rabbit' is being conceptualised as a mass, not a concrete, individual animal.

Some things, like 'rabbit', can be conceptualised either way: think of how your mental image changes if you have eaten 'too *much* chocolate' (mass) or 'too *many* chocolates' (individual countable items), or even 'too *much* rabbit' (mass) or 'too *many* rabbits' (individual countable items). We return to this topic in more detail in Chapter 4.

English grammatical rules, such as this one about how to quantify mass and countable items, might be found in other languages, but they might not. A multitude of rules governing the classification of objects is possible. In Chinese languages, objects are classified according to whether they are long or short, while in some Australian aboriginal languages, objects are classified according to whether or not they are dangerous. Many meanings – like mass/countable, dangerous/safe – can be encoded into a grammar, but the meanings that are encoded and those that are not vary from culture to culture, and the descriptive grammarian should be aware of this fact, and expect diversity.

Accounting for Language Change

So far we have considered different languages and different dialects of a single language, but even a single variety can change over time. English and Scots have changed quite substantially over the past millennium. An example of this is the virtual loss of the subjunctive mood in contemporary English, a topic that is covered in Chapter 9 of this book. A descriptive grammarian looks at the ways that grammatical patterns encode meanings in earlier versions of the language, and tries to relate these earlier patterns of structure and meaning to present-day usage.

Theories of Grammar

It would be a mistake to assume that the grammar of English is somehow 'out there', waiting to be discovered. A grammar, after all, is a human construction, and people make things in different ways for different reasons. Consequently, there are many grammars of English. However, all grammars of English assume that the language is structured, that it is governed by rules that account for the ordering of certain *constituents* – that is, bits and pieces of language – so that they make sense. But, after that, theories of grammar can diverge quite markedly. Some grammarians are mainly concerned with finding valid methods for discovering the acceptable and unacceptable patterns of a particular language. Their hope is that if you apply these methods to given linguistic data, a comprehensive profile of the structures used in the language should become clear. Since these grammars are concerned with structures, they are called *structuralist* grammars.

Other grammarians have different agendas. Some assume that language is the result of an instinct, of a natural predisposition to speak, which is part of the mental make-up of every normal human being. These grammarians believe that if they can devise a set of rules that will not simply describe but also generate acceptable sentences, then they will have discovered a model not just of language, but of a basic human mental process. Such grammarians devise abstract and complex rules that will generate sentences and transform one sentence into another. These sets of rules are called *transformational-generative* grammars. They are associated particularly with the American thinker Noam Chomsky, one of the best-known intellectuals of the present day, famous for his political as well as his linguistic writings.

Since the 1970s, *cognitive grammar* has been associated with a group of American linguists, including Wallace Chafe, Charles Fillmore, George Lakoff and Ronald Langacker. Cognitive grammar theorises about the psychological bases of linguistic structures. Unlike those who work in the Chomskyan tradition, cognitive grammarians focus less on devising rules that generate grammatical structures, and more on the ways that grammatical structures encode meanings.

A further set of grammarians views language as a vast and complicated system of choices. The choices made by a speaker are selected in order to accomplish a particular function in a given social context. *Systemic-functional* grammarians are interested in making models of the language system, and explaining how linguistic choices are related to sets of social functions. These grammars are associated particularly with the linguist Michael Halliday, whose work became influential from the 1960s onwards, particularly in Britain and Australia.

More recently, *corpus* grammarians such as Mike McCarthy and Ronald Carter have followed pioneers such as John Sinclair, and used vast electronic archives of contemporary speech and writing to devise accounts of English that are 'driven by the data', not by grammatical theories. The present book is a modest contribution to this new tradition in descriptive linguistics.

One result of all this grammatical theorising is that no two grammar books are exactly the same. This fact is often frustrating for the beginner, who picks up one book to try to clarify an obscure point in another, only to find that a whole new set of approaches and jargon has to be learnt. There is no easy answer to this problem – with time and experience, though, the basic principles of grammatical analysis will become more familiar to you, and the theoretical assumptions of other writers on grammar should fall more readily into place.

This book does not seek to discuss grammatical theories. Although we draw upon certain models of language as the basis of our analyses, in this book we aim to guide the beginner in a set of techniques that will help him or her to identify parts of speech and analyse fairly simple sentences. This process of identification and analysis is traditionally called 'parsing', and parsing is the focus of the first part of this book.

1.3   Applying Grammatical Knowledge

Some people are interested in describing grammar not for its own sake, but in order to apply it to related disciplines, such as literary studies. Grammatical description is crucial to the procedures used in those human sciences that demand precise descriptions of communicative behaviour, for example literary and media studies, history, sociology, education, and philosophy. A literary critic, for example, will use his or her knowledge of grammatical analysis to explore how a writer chooses to make meanings, and s/he will be able to draw upon this grammatical knowledge to give a detailed account of how meanings are constructed in literary texts. Many modern poems use repeated grammatical structures as the basis of the line of verse; one such poem is Edwin Morgan's 'A View of Things'.

(For an electronic version of this text, see the Scottish Poetry Library's website: www.edwinmorgan.spl.org.uk/poems/view_of_things.html).

A View of Things

what I love about dormice is their size
what I hate about rain is its sneer
what I love about Bratach Gorm is its unflappability
what I hate about scent is its smell

Morgan's poem can be discussed in several ways; one approach would be to look at its grammar. Each line of the poem is a complete grammatical unit, alternating as follows:

what I love about A is its B
what I hate about C is its D

As the poem progresses in a series of complete grammatical units expressing the speaker's love or hate of the unpredictable features of apparently random things, the reader begins to build up a fuller, very idiosyncratic 'view of things'. In other words, the reader begins to see the world through the eyes of another, rather quirky, persona. This destabilisation of perspectives is one of the pleasures of much modern poetry.

But there is another characteristic of the grammatical choice that gives each line of this poem its characteristic structure. The opening lines of the poem could be rewritten as:

I love the size of dormice
I hate the sneer of rain

So what is the difference between the grammatical choice of:

I love the B of A

and

What I love about A is its B

The answer is that the latter type of grammatical construction expresses a sense of *exclusivity* – the implication is that, for the speaker or writer, the *only* or *most important* thing about dormice is their size. The former, less exclusive, construction allows the speaker or writer to say 'I love the size of dormice…amongst many other things I love about them'. The poet needs the exclusivity of the 'what I love/hate about A…' structure, in order to press home the individual strangeness of his view of things.

Meanings, then, depend on grammatical choices. We can explore grammatical choices in many ways, one of the most productive being rephrasing utterances to show what other choices are possible. Another – very powerful – way of exploring grammar and meaning is to take a grammatical unit, strip it down to its essential components, and then examine how these components combine to make sense. That skill is what this book seeks to teach.

1.4   Discussion Topics

By now you should have a clear idea of what is meant by a descriptive and prescriptive grammar, you should be aware of the aims of this book, and you should be able to give some possible reasons why a basic understanding of grammar can be useful, even fascinating! Before we start looking in more detail at the techniques of grammatical description we are going to encounter in this book, consider the following passages, (i) to (iv), and then try some simple SCOTS corpus searches.

Attitudes to grammar
Texts (i-iv) are a collection of statements about English grammar, made by a variety of commentators. Look back at the general meanings of 'grammar' discussed above, and decide which meaning (if any!) these commentators assume that their readers share. Do you agree with their arguments?

(i)   Norman Tebbit, politician (1985), quoted in D. Graddol & J. Swann (1988) 'Trapping Linguists' in *Language and Education,* 2, pp. 95-111

If you allow standards to slip to the stage where good English is no better than bad English, where people turn up filthy…at school…all those things tend to cause people to have no standards at all, and once you lose standards then there's no imperative to stay out of crime.

(ii)   John Simon, theatre and film reviewer (1980), quoted in S. Pinker (1994) *The Language Instinct* London: Penguin. Simon is writing on Black English Vernacular:

Why should we consider some, usually poorly educated, subculture's notion of the relationship between sound and meaning? And how could a grammar – any grammar – possibly describe that relationship?

As for 'I be', 'you be', 'he be', etc., which should give us all the heebie-jeebies, these may indeed be comprehensible, but they go against all accepted classical and modern grammars and are the product not of a language with roots in history but of ignorance of how language works.

(iii) John Rae, headmaster of Westminster School (1982), quoted in J. & L. Milroy (1985), *Authority in Language* London: Routledge

The overthrow of grammar coincided with the acceptance of the equivalent of creative writing in social behaviour. As nice points of grammar were mockingly dismissed as pedantic and irrelevant, so was punctiliousness in such matters as honesty, responsibility, property, gratitude, apology, and so on.

(iv) Anthony Lejune, letter to the *Daily Telegraph* (1985), quoted in V. Shephard (1990) *Language Variety and the Art of the Everyday* London: Pinter

...a language teacher at the University of Bath...wrote that standard (i.e.) correct English has no 'inherent superiority'. But it has. Correct grammar and syntax and the accurate use of words derive not only from history and custom but from logic. They are the mortar which holds our thoughts together. When they crumble, so does our capacity for thought.

1.5 Some Basic Corpus Searches

Let's say that you wished to use the SCOTS corpus to investigate the use of standard and non-standard occurrences of a particular expression, such as 'I saw/seen'.

The quickest way is to go to www.scottishcorpus.ac.uk and type the expression you wish to look at in the 'Standard Search' menu.

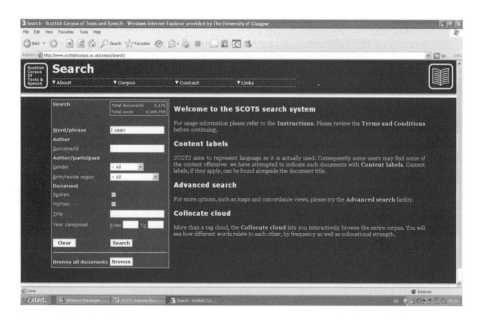

This search will look for all instances of 'I seen' in the 4-million word corpus, including all spoken and written documents. The results page will look something like this (as the corpus is periodically updated, results may change from time to time):

The results for this search show that the sequence 'I seen' appears in 25 documents in the corpus, ranging from spontaneous speech to a written diary and parliamentary proceedings. However, on closer inspection, several documents mentioned can be discounted, since 'I seen' appears not only as a variant of 'I saw' but as part of a larger, formal inverted construction, where 'have/had' appears before the 'I'. This is also true of several of the written documents listed, e.g.

20. **Never have *I seen* a bruised face like it.**
21. **nor had *I seen* the newspaper report.**
22. **What visions have *I seen*!**

Of the remaining documents, some are written documents that happen to be first-person narratives in Broad Scots:

23. **Yon red squirrel *I seen* speed across the Muchty road.**
24. **it wis aa chokit up wi growth, an *I seen* desertit it for e parks.**

Example (24) looks decidedly odd, and, sure enough, on closer inspection it is clear that this text is not only in Broad Scots, but it is written in North-East Scots. Example (24) gives an instance of southern 'oo' becoming 'ee': the sense is that the speaker *soon* deserted a cart-track for the fields.

The remaining examples of 'I seen' are either in spontaneous speech or in the dialogue of fictional narratives. By far the most common occurrence of 'I seen' in a single document is in one of the recordings of spontaneous speech, between two students conversing about leisure activities. Here the expression occurs five times, roughly 0.51 times per 1000 words:

25. **Oh right, *I I seen* there was a message on your phone**
26. **I was quite annoyed, but erm *I seen* like this huge big punchbag**
27. **and I went in and *I seen* the the tenner**
28. **and *I seen* them pullin the wee barriers across**
29. **And then *I seen* the guy**

Let's now compare this search with a similar search for 'I saw'. A standard search finds the results shown below. There are many more instances of 'I saw' than 'I seen' in the SCOTS corpus as a whole. 'I saw' currently appears 127 times in 79 documents, i.e. in fiction, spontaneous conversation, personal letters, email correspondence, weblogs and parliamentary proceedings. 'I saw' appears in documents in Broad Scots as well as in English, in dialogue as well as in narrative sections of text. A few of the occurrences are as follows. Examples (30) to (33) are written, and examples (34) to (36) are from recordings of speech.

30. **suddenly *I saw* the British educational policy for the next four years**
31. ***I saw* the STOP programme when we visited the unit in Barlinnie**
32. **As I cam doon bi Ythanside *I saw* a fruit bat hingin**
33. **because *I saw* how much agony I was puttin him through**
34. **And eh [tut] *I saw* an advert in the Courier office**
35. **you know, *I saw* the two things side by side**

What observations, then, can we make from these two simple searches, intended to compare the use of 'I saw' and 'I seen'? The first, obviously, is that searches cannot be purely mechanical. Of the 25 apparent instances of 'I seen' in the SCOTS corpus, three have to be discarded since they are part of the formal construction 'have/had I seen' and not therefore variants of 'I saw'. One further instance of 'seen' is a phonetic spelling of the North-East Scots pronunciation of 'soon'. So we only have 21 instances of 'I seen' in the archive. Many of these instances are in a single document, a spontaneous conversation between two students, and the others occur in speech or written dialogue. 'I seen', therefore, is strongly associated with speech in Scotland, and despite the fact that it can appear frequently in the conversation of some speakers, it is still relatively infrequent when compared to 'I saw'.

'I saw' is very much more frequent than 'I seen', occurring five times for each occurrence of 'I seen'. It is not confined to speech or the written representation of speech, and it even occurs in Broad Scots speech and writing. It occurs in a wide range of written genres. In general, the evidence suggests that it is the preferred form in Scotland.

Do these results mean that 'I seen' is *wrong*? The descriptive linguist would resist framing the question in terms of absolute rightness or wrongness. Rather, he or she would point to the evidence and indicate that 'I seen' is used by a minority of speakers in informal conversation, and by writers of fiction who wish to represent informal conversation. The speakers who use it in these cases use it relatively frequently, but consistently and meaningfully. Its use possibly signals an aspect of their personal identity – at some level of consciousness they may wish to distance themselves from the formal norms preferred by the education system, or they may simply wish to sound informal and friendly. But 'I seen' is very infrequent outside the context of informal speech. Compared to 'I saw' its use in formal writing in the SCOTS corpus is negligible. These kinds of results allow the descriptive linguist to suggest that the use of 'I seen' outside speech would be *inappropriate*. But, since the descriptive linguist is also a cautious animal, he or she would add the proviso that attitudes to language do gradually shift. If more speakers wish to mark their personal identity by using 'I seen', then its use will probably expand from informal to more formal speech, and from speech to writing. If that occurs, 'I seen' would be regarded as 'correct' and 'I saw' as old-fashioned, or even 'quaint'.

1.6 Activity

One change in the language that is currently happening relates to certain words like 'team' and 'class' that can be thought of as either singular or plural; that is, we can say:

> The team or class *is*...
> The team or class *are*...

Look at the Standard Search menu for the SCOTS corpus at www.scottishcorpus.ac.uk and try to figure out which is the preferred form in today's Scotland. You can use the Standard Search menu to restrict your search to spoken or written documents, and compare results. Remember to treat the raw results with care!

Scottish Corpus Of Texts & Speech

Search

▼ About   ▼ Corpus   ▼ Contact   ▼ Links

| Search | Total documents | 1,176 |
| | Total words | 4,049,755 |

Word/phrase   team is

Author
Surname/id

Author/participant
Gender   - All
Birth/reside region   - All

Document
Spoken   ☑
Written   ■
Title
Year composed   From   To

Clear   Search

Browse all documents   Browse

Welcome to the SCOTS search system

For usage information please refer to the **Instructions**. Please review the **Terms and Conditions** before continuing.

Content labels

SCOTS aims to represent language as it is actually used. Consequently some users may find some of the content offensive: we have attempted to indicate such documents with **Content labels**. Content labels, if they apply, can be found alongside the document title.

Advanced search

For more options, such as maps and concordance views, please try the **Advanced search** facility.

Collocate cloud

More than a tag cloud, the **Collocate cloud** lets you interactively browse the entire corpus. You will see how different words relate to each other, by frequency as well as collocational strength.

Chapter 2   Identifying Parts Of Speech

2.0   About this Chapter

This Chapter begins to focus on the basic principles of grammatical analysis, otherwise known as 'parsing'. First, we give a brief overview of different levels of grammatical structure (sentence – clause – phrase – word – morpheme). Then we consider in more detail the three criteria used to classify grammatical units – namely *meaning, form* and *function* – by looking at how these criteria combine in the classification of different kinds of word.

2.1   What is 'Parsing', and Why do They Say Such Terrible Things about It?

The process of taking a sentence and breaking it down into ever smaller units of structure is traditionally called 'parsing'. A glance at the citations given for this word in the *Oxford English Dictionary* gives a sense of how parsing has been viewed over the centuries. Its first recorded appearance in the English language is in a text called *The Schoolmaster,* published around 1568, and early references are to the identification of grammatical items in Latin and Greek, as well as in English. By 1908, L. M. Montgomery is writing, in the classic Canadian children's novel, *Anne of Green Gables,* that 'They had studied Tennyson's poem in school the preceding winter... They had analyzed and parsed it and torn it to pieces in general'. Montgomery's scepticism about the value of analysis, parsing and 'generally tearing to pieces' is clear, and anticipates a general turn against such practices later in the 20th century. As the OED citations show, by 1992 the *New York Times Book Review* can state that 'It has been a very long time since anyone parsed a sentence in public'. Scotland is not alone, then, in having displaced parsing from its central role in English teaching; however, there are many arguments in favour of reconsidering its value.

That said, there is no escape from the fact that parsing is a subtle and demanding practice. Of course it can be done tediously and mechanically, without sensitivity to the ways in which utterances and sentences convey meanings in context. Moreover, like most complex and rigorous practices, parsing can inspire fear in those who have not been initiated into its mysteries. However, given some systematic practice, if the meaning of examples is taken into consideration, parsing can be an accessible, useful and even empowering skill. This Chapter shows you how to begin to acquire it.

Let us take, for example, a sentence uttered by a young child to her father. (As usual, the illustrations in **bold type** are taken from actual utterances or writings recorded in the SCOTS corpus. Examples are numbered within each Chapter.)

1. **Yes I am quite good at drawing, because I can draw a little funny face!**

Even at her early stage of development, this child has mastered a sentence that is made up of two units, which we will shortly learn to call *clauses*:

(a) **Yes I am quite good at drawing** (b) **because I can draw a little funny face!**

Each of these clauses, in turn, is made up of a sequence of *phrases*. Note that the technical use of the term 'phrase' in grammatical analysis differs slightly from its more general use. 'Phrase' generally means *more than one word*, whereas, when performing a grammatical analysis, we take a phrase to be *one or more* related words. For reasons that will soon be explained, the words 'Yes' and 'because' fall outside the boundaries of any phrase, and so the child's utterance can be further broken down as:

Yes (i) **I** (ii) **am** (iii) **quite good** (iv) **at drawing**

because (v) **I** (vi) **can draw** (vii) **a little funny face!**

Phrases, in their turn, are made up of individual words:

Yes + I + am + quite + good + at + drawing + because + I + can + draw + a + little + funny + face!

We could take our grammatical analysis one step further and look at the little grammatical units that make up words, namely 'morphemes'. For example, we could further divide *drawing* into two morphemes: *draw + ing*. Morphemes are the smallest unit of grammar. Some words, like *good,* consist of a single morpheme, while others are made up of two or more. Therefore, when we consider grammar as a whole, we can think of morphemes combining to make words; words combining to make phrases; phrases

22

combining to make clauses; and clauses combining to make sentences. Much of the rest of this book is concerned with how these different kinds of combination occur. Sentences are the upper limit of grammatical analysis. When we want to consider the organisation of language beyond the sentence, we have to enter the realm of *discourse*. When considering discourse, for example, we would look at the above child's utterance and consider its status as an answer to her father's question.

In this Chapter we shall confine ourselves to learning the basic principles that we use when assigning grammatical labels to parts of speech. Greater detail about these labels is given in later Chapters. In this Chapter, the examples primarily illustrate *how* the classification of any given sentence into clauses, phrases, words and morphemes is achieved. Although these general principles of classification can be used at all levels within the sentence, we will focus here mainly on *words*.

A reasonable opening question is: 'How do we attach a grammatical label to words?' After all, we know that there are different kinds of word, e.g. nouns, verbs, prepositions, adverbs, articles, conjunctions, and so on. What criteria are used to decide what kind of word any given example is? The answer is that there are certain *tests* that you will learn in the course of this book which help us to decide.

In general, these tests consider three things: the *meaning, form* and *function* of a grammatical unit such as a word, phrase or clause. The consideration of the meaning, form and function of any grammatical unit should give sufficient information to assign a label to it. Often, it is not sufficient to consider one of these criteria alone. The task of labelling might well rely on the consideration of all three. Let us look at some examples.

2.2   Meaning

When grammar is taught at the early stages in school, teachers might well direct pupils to use the *meaning* of an item to classify it. Consequently, a 'thing' or an 'object', like *table,* is classified as a *noun,* while a 'doing word' or an 'action', like *run,* is classified as a *verb.* 'Describing words' like *red* or *ugly* can be classified as *adjectives*, while those words which describe verbs, like *quickly* or *slowly,* are *adverbs*.

The criterion of meaning can certainly be useful when labelling words and phrases, but it is not in itself sufficient to deal with all the complexities of grammar. Consider a few of the problems of using meaning alone to classify words.

First, consider the word 'baby'. If asked to classify this word, you might say, 'It's an object, a thing. Therefore it must be a noun'. And you would be correct. A quick glance at a list of examples of 'baby' and 'babies' in the SCOTS corpus shows that young people or certain things are meant by the uses of these words in context, e.g.

2. **if you're pushing a baby in a pram**
3. **that was worse than having a baby**
4. **eating chocolate babies (or soldiers)**
5. **soft as the toes of babies**

However, even though we seem to be able to use meaning to label the vast majority of examples of 'baby'/'babies' as 'things' and therefore 'nouns', there will usually be exceptions that are difficult to account for. Consider the uses of 'baby' and 'babies' in the following short text, taken from a container of talcum powder:

6. Nobody babies you better than Johnson's

While in the examples from the SCOTS corpus we can classify 'baby' and 'babies' as nouns, in the heading of the advertisement for talcum powder, 'babies' is a 'doing word', and can therefore be classed as a verb: 'Nobody *babies* you better...'. It can even be turned into a past action: 'She *babied* me better than you!'

Worse, in examples (7) and (8) below, 'baby' seems to be some kind of decribing word. Is it therefore an adjective?

7. **I did remember to put *baby* oil on his tender parts**
8. **that's a *baby* kind of capital A**

In brief, the examples show that the meaning of 'baby' is inconveniently variable: the word can indeed refer to a thing, a young child, but it can also refer to treating someone as if he or she were a child, in other words pampering them, and it can even mean 'for a baby' (in 'baby oil') or just plain small ('a baby kind of capital A'). If meaning were our *only* criterion for classification, then, we would be having serious problems by now. So what other criteria can we use to add to that of meaning?

2.3 Form

The 'form' of a grammatical constituent is simply those elements which make it up. As noted above, the smallest grammatical elements are called *morphemes*, and these combine to make *words*. Morphemes can be classified

24

generally into root morphemes (e.g. *beauty*), to which different *affixes* might be added (e.g. *beauti-ful, beauti-cian*). We can classify some words according to the type of morpheme which they contain, particularly affixes. For example, words which have affixes like *–cian* tend to be nouns, while those words which end in *–ful* tend to be adjectives. We can do a 'wild card' search of the SCOTS corpus for words ending in *–cian* by keying in ***cian**. To do this, you can do the following:

(a) Go to www.scottishcorpus.ac.uk
(b) Click on Advanced Search.
(c) Click on General, then Word Search, and then Word/phrase (concordance).
(d) Type *cian into the box that appears and press Return.
(e) When the results appear, scroll down the page and look at the concordance.
(f) Repeat the process for *ful.

Sure enough, all the English words found in the concordance are nouns: **clinician, dietician, electrician, magician, mathematician, mortician, musician, optician, phonetician, physician, politician, rhetorician, technician**.

Most – but not all – of the words found by searching ***ful** are adjectives, e.g. **awful, baleful, bashful, beautiful, blissful, bountiful, careful, cheerful, colourful, deceitful, disgraceful, doubtful, dreadful, dutiful, faithful**, and so on. A smaller group of '-ful' words are nouns that signify a quantity of something, e.g. **an armful of mist, a basketful, a beakful of goodies, a big bowlful of soup, a carful of... lobsters, a cupful of milk**. Again, the form of the latter group is a clue to their grammatical nature: they are made up of two morphemes, the first signifying some kind of container (arm, basket, beak, bowl, car, cup, etc.) and the second being 'ful'.

Other types of formal criteria are fairly reliable in distinguishing other classes of word. For example, *adverbs* very often end in *–ly*. A concordance search of ***ly** in the SCOTS corpus includes the following among many other examples of adverbs:

9. **Haiku are *normally* restricted to three lines**
10. **to emerge from the *partly* clogged-up nozzle**
11. **some rustic scrivener *painstakingly* describes every detail**
12. **'Och tae heck wi this,' he said oot *loudly*.**
13. ***Unfortunately,* the varied club events lost some of their individuality**

All the italicised words in examples (9) to (13) end in *–ly*. This formal similarity corresponds with certain patterns of meaning and use. Some of the words tell us how people perform actions (*painstakingly, loudly*). Some of the words describe other descriptive words (*normally restricted, partly clogged up*). One of the words gives a sense of how the writer feels about the incident he is writing about (*Unfortunately…*). These three functions are associated with different kinds of adverb. However, form, like meaning, is not an absolutely reliable criterion for classification. The SCOTS corpus also includes the following words ending in *–ly* whose form therefore suggests they are adverbs. However, in meaning and use, they are clearly something else, e.g.

14. **Anderson Casey's a bit of a *wally***
15. **That's *lovely* dear**
16. **a mane of *steely* hair**

Although these three italicised words also end with *–ly,* they are not adverbs. The first is an evocative word for a certain kind of person; it is therefore a noun. The second and third are descriptive words in their own right; they are both adjectives. As well as the form of grammatical items, we have to consider the criteria of meaning and usage. There are also adverbs, such as *fast, quite* and *well,* that do not end with *–ly.*

Despite the exceptions, form is important because it is still one of the most reliable means of classifying grammatical items. For example, *verbs* can easily be identified because they have a far greater range of forms than, say, *nouns* (which tend only to have two forms, a singular and a plural, such as *chair, chair**s*** or *child, child**ren***). Certain kinds of word in English are invariant, that is their forms do not change at all – this is true of adverbs such as *slowly.* Verbs are easily recognisable because their form changes a lot, for example according to who is performing the action (*I speak/she speaks*), or according to the tense of the action (*I enjoy/I enjoyed).* The irregular verb *to be* is an extreme example of this, since it changes its form according to person and number (I/we, you, he/she/it/they) as well as tense (past and present):

Forms of the verb 'to be'

Present	Past	Other forms
I *am*	I/he/she/it *was*	I have *been*
You/we/they *are*	You/we/they *were*	We are *being*
He/she/it *is*		

To recap, then, formal criteria are a good way of identifying word classes. Words in the same grammatical category tend to change their forms in similar ways. However, there are problems if you want to use formal criteria alone to categorise words. As noted above, there are exceptions to most of the rules. Not all words that end with –*ly* are adverbs, and not all adverbs end with –*ly,* for example. Moreover, certain words, like *and, if, with, the* and *for,* never change their form at all, yet they do not all belong to the same grammatical class. And there are irregular words, like the verb *to be,* that change their forms in idiosyncratic ways.

Like tests of meaning, then, formal tests give us *some* guidance when we are labelling grammatical constituents, but we need other criteria if we are to deal with the various exceptions to the formal 'rules' and with different parts of speech.

2.4   Function

'Function' is one of those words which has different meanings in different grammatical and linguistic theories. Sometimes it refers to the uses to which a sentence is put – for example, whether it is asking a question, making a statement, or giving a command. Here, however, we will use 'function' in a narrower sense, to mean *the relationship between grammatical constituents.*

There are undeniably rules governing the relationship between words. These rules tell a native speaker that an expression like *a fast car* is acceptable, while *a fast very is unacceptable. Consider, for a moment, the relationship between the three words in the phrase

a fast car.

The most important word in this phrase is obviously *car*. The other two words tell us something about it. *Fast* describes it, and *a*, more vaguely, perhaps, tells us that this car belongs to a set of items which might be new to the speaker. (Compare the expression *the fast car,* i.e. the car I expect that you already know about.)

In short, both *a* and *fast* modify the meaning of *car* in different ways. Both, then, are labelled *modifiers* of the *headword,* which in this instance is *car.*

Different parts of speech have different types of modifiers and headwords. For example, if you run a concordance for *car* in the SCOTS corpus, and then list the items on the left of the key-word, or *node*, you find that certain words and types of word re-occur. First there are modifying words such as *a, another, the, this* and *that.* Then there are descriptive words – adjectives – such as *American, old, burnt-out, clammy, clean, damaged* among many others. Words, therefore, tend to combine in fairly regular patterns, and so we can use these patterns of combination to describe individual units. It is a little like labelling someone not according to his or her own gender, ethnicity or age, but according to the company he or she keeps.

Phrases, as well as individual words, enter into functional relationships with other grammatical constituents, and these relationships can help define them. This fact can be illustrated by the following sentence:

17a. **The child read them out as part of the story.**

– and its reformulation:

17b. They were read out by the child as part of the story.

Here we might wish to identify the phrase that functions as the grammatical Subject of each sentence. One possible way of identifying the Subject is to define it simply as the person or thing doing the action. However, in (17a) and (17b) above, the person or thing doing the action is clearly *the child.* However, *the child* is not the Subject of (17b). How then do we identify the Subject of sentence (17b)? The answer is that there is a relationship between the Subject and the verb phrase of these sentences (the verb phrase is *read* in (17a) and *were read* in (17b)). This relationship determines that if the Subject is singular in number, then the verb phrase is also singular; but if the Subject is plural then the verb phrase is also plural. This functional relationship is called *concord* or *agreement.* Let's consider how it applies to sentences (17a) and (17b).

In sentence (17a) the verb *read* is in the past tense, and so unfortunately is not marked for number. However, if we cheat a little and change it to present tense, we can easily see that it has to agree with the Subject – compare *the child reads* (singular) and *the children read* (plural).

In sentence (17b) the verb is plural because the Subject is plural **(they were** **read)**. When we change the Subject so that it is singular, we also have to change the form of the verb **(it was read)**. We can use this relationship between Subject and verb phrase, then, to give a *functional* definition of the Subject: the Subject is that part of speech which has a relationship of concord or agreement with the verb phrase. So in (17a) the Subject is *the child,* and in (17b) the subject is *they.*

2.5   Putting it All Together

As we have seen, none of the three criteria used for classifying parts of speech – meaning, form and function – is particularly reliable on its own. However, if used together, they can help us determine what classes grammatical constituents belong to. Even then, there will be grey areas and ambiguities when we encounter actual speech and non-standard usages: language is after all a dynamic thing and the categories and classes change over time. Often these changes involve a part of speech shifting from one class into another. For example, we can take a look at the results of a SCOTS corpus search for the word 'well'. A selection of concordance lines shows that this word works in different ways in different contexts. Sometimes, but remarkably rarely, it is used as an adjective, a descriptive word that relates to a noun or noun phrase:

18. **Hope all is *well.***
19. **I wasn't feelin *well*, I was feelin sick…**

More often, it is used as an adverb, either an *adverb of manner,* that is the kind of adverb that tells you how an action is being performed (i.e. well or badly) –

20. **Today's lesson went *well.***
21. **I remember it *well.***

– or as an *intensifier,* that is the kind of adverb that intensifies the meaning of the following adjective:

22. **the Maori girls were *well* built and friendly**
23. **all MSPs are *well* aware of that vital contribution**
24. **the embankment itself is *well* overgrown**

In recent years, for certain speakers 'well' has been used more broadly as an intensifying adverb in expressions like 'That's well wicked,' or 'He's well up for it'. Not everyone uses 'well' in this way; such expressions tend to suggest youthfulness or a pose of informality:

25. **spiked up like the singer from the *well* cool band they all liked**

Other uses in the SCOTS corpus give evidence of 'well' as a noun:

26. **Morag sits down at the edge of the *well***

And, of course, amongst other uses, 'well' is often found as a 'filler' or 'hesitation marker' often at or near the beginning of spoken utterances. This kind of 'well' has several functions; e.g. it might indicate that it is a speaker's turn to contribute to a conversation, or that the same speaker has started a new topic (or is returning to a previous one after a digression). In other situations, and depending on the intonation, 'well' might indicate qualified agreement with the person you are talking to. This 'discourse signalling' function of 'well' is in fact one of the most common uses in the SCOTS corpus:

27. **Well, when I did, I did the Indian head massage**
28. **Well, we were sittin, on the side o the road, the two o us**
29. **Yeah, *well*, aye**

However, even given the fact that a single word can have many uses and that its meanings shift, a consideration of the meaning, form and function of a word should help you to classify it reliably. In Chapter 3 we embark upon a more extensive description of word classes. Particularly when new words are introduced in the sections that follow, bear in mind the three criteria for classification, and consider how they are being used to assign a word to its particular group.

2.6   Review Activities: Thinking about Meaning, Form and Function

Activity 1
Literary language often deviates from standard English in interesting and thought-provoking ways. At one extreme lies 'nonsense' poetry such as 'Jabberwocky', the beginning of which is reprinted below. Though many of the words in the poem do not in fact exist, their grammatical categories can be deduced from (i) their *form* (e.g. their grammatical endings), and (ii) the way they *function* in relation to the 'normal' words around them. In this way, their *meanings* can be guessed at generally, even if they cannot be tied down specifically.

'Jabberwocky' by Lewis Carroll

'Twas brillig, and the slithy toves
    Did gyre and gimble in the wabe:
All mimsy were the borogoves,
    And the mome raths outgrabe.

Write down a list of five 'real' English words which could be substituted for each of the following words in the poem, so that it makes more obvious sense:

     slithy   *gimble*   *raths*   *outgrabe*

1.

2.

3.

4.

5.

Now look at the 'substitute words' that you have written. Which category of words do they belong to? What does this tell you about the category of *slithy, gimble, raths* and *outgrabe*? (If you are unsure about grammatical classification, use a dictionary to help you with this activity. The dictionary will indicate whether a word is a noun, verb, adjective, adverb, etc.)

Note that this substitution activity might help you if you are unsure about the classification of words later in this book. If, for example, you are unsure about how to classify 'serious' in a sentence like '**they were also serious Communist lefties by their way of it**' then try substituting the word with others that you do know how to classify, e.g. 'they were also *poor /unhappy/frivolous/dedicated/mad* Communist lefties'.

If all the others are, say, adjectives (as is the case here), then there is a good chance that the word you don't know is an adjective too.

Activity 2
Below you can see the information about Johnson's Baby Powder taken from a Brazilian container. Note that the Portuguese is not a direct translation of an English version! Even without knowing the language, it should still be possible to read the Portuguese and make some observations about:

(a)   the *form* of the Portuguese words – how can the form help you to identify nouns, verbs, adjectives, etc? How do you think the plural is formed in Portuguese? What is the formal relationship between adjectives and nouns?

(b)   the *function* of the Portuguese words – e.g. does the order of
         adjectives and nouns correspond to English patterns?

(c)   the *meanings* of the words. Having identified the grammatical
         category of as many items as you can, how much of the text can you
         understand?

> O **Talco Johnson's baby** é feito com o talco
> da mais alta qualidade e pureza, que junto
> com sua exclusiva fragrância, deixa a pele
> suave, macia e perfumada, protegendo-a
> contra o atrito e umidade que podem causar
> assaduras e irritações.

Activity 3
Look at the following examples from the SCOTS corpus of incidences of the
word 'fast'. Consider its meaning, form and function in each example, and
try classifying each use of the word:

1.   **They were gaining on us fast.**
2.   **The kids are growing up fast.**
3.   **Holy Mary, he's intae the fast lane again.**
4.   **The kirk session would hold a fast on Pace Sunday.**
5.   **Time is fast running out.**
6.   **It was a fast three weeks.**
7.   **yin by yin we aa fell fast asleep.**
8.   **the chance to mak a fast buck.**
9.   **popping into a fast food place for a welcome kebab.**
10.   **I had to get the hell out of there. Fast!**

The form of 'fast' does not vary, but if you substitute another word for 'fast'
in some cases, the form of the substitute word varies – and that can act as a
clue to categorise 'fast'. Think too of which words 'fast' combines with in
the examples given above, and how the meaning of 'fast' changes from
example to example.

Chapter 3   Describing Words

3.0   About this Chapter

This Chapter continues the introduction to parsing begun in Chapter 2 by giving an overview of the types of word found in English and Scots. Like most grammarians, we group some of these word-types in broader categories. Here, in particular, we focus on the 'open' and 'closed' categories of words. These categories are always based on meaning, form and function, as discussed in the previous Chapter. In this Chapter we also introduce eleven basic word types; in Chapter 4 we discuss the major categories in more detail.

3.1   Identifying Word Classes

In the previous Chapter, we considered the principles of assigning grammatical labels to word classes like 'noun', 'verb', 'adjective', and so on. In this Chapter, we shall apply these principles to a much more detailed survey of English word classes.

We saw in the preceding Chapter that words can be classified according to their meaning, form and function. For example, the members of one set of words tend to refer to *things* (that is their meaning); they generally have two *forms*, namely singular and plural; and they are often preceded by words like 'my/this/that/a/the' (that is, these are the words they *function* alongside). We call all those words that exhibit these characteristics 'nouns'. The members of another set tend to refer to actions or states, they have a variety of forms depending, for example, on whether they refer to present or past events, and they are preceded by words like 'is/was/has/have/can/could'. We label this set of items 'verbs'.

In general, sets of English words can be divided into two groups, the *open* and *closed* word classes. The basis for this classification is a simple one: some types of word carry most of the meaning of a sentence, and we can easily add new words of these types to the language. Other sets of words play more of a supporting role, and so they behave differently and are more resistant to change.

For example, new nouns and adjectives are always being coined or borrowed from other languages, and then used and sometimes discarded. Teenage slang is a fruitful source of new coinages, as we can see in the term 'grunge', recorded in the SCOTS corpus, for example, in the following utterance:

1. **the teen phenomenon of** *grunge*

According to the *Oxford English Dictionary*, 'grungy' is first recorded in American slang, as an adjective meaning 'untidy', 'dirty' or 'unappealing', in the mid 1960s. The noun expressing the quality of 'grunginess' first appears in Canada in the late 1970s. At the start of that decade, 'grunge' also appears as a noun expressing:

> a style of rock music characterized by a raucous, often discordant guitar sound, lazy vocal delivery, and downbeat, freq. nihilistic lyrics, and (in later use) influenced by heavy metal and punk rock.

If a word-class can accept new members, then, like the class of nouns or adjectives, it is an *open word-class.*

The *closed word-classes,* however, do not accept new members so willingly. One example is the class of pronouns (a class that includes *I/me, you, he/him, she/her, it, we/us, they/them*). In principle, these sets of words *could* be added to – but change is extremely difficult to accomplish. For example, some people have argued that English suffers from not having a gender-neutral pronoun with the meaning 'he or she' and 'him or her' to use in sentences like 'Everybody knows what he or she should do'. It would be quite easy to invent a word which would do this – e.g. 'shim', as in 'Everybody knows what *shim* [i.e. he/she] should do', but although some attempts have been made to rectify this politically incorrect deficiency in English grammar, they have not been generally accepted. This is because the closed word-classes are much more resistant to innovation than the open word-classes. This resistance to change is actually because these two types of word-class perform different tasks in English grammar (see further, 3.2 below).

The frequency of open and closed-class items in the language is also different. The five most frequent words in the SCOTS corpus, at the time of writing, are *the, to, of, and,* and *a.* The most frequent, *the,* occurs 224,089 times in the 4 million or so words (at the time of writing). *Of* occurs 78,992 times. Among the least frequent words – those that currently only appear once in the entire corpus – are *carcase* and *husky,* alongside the Broad Scots terms *pingilt, whotten* and *panshit*. All the frequent words are closed-class items; all the infrequent ones are open-class. To understand the reasons for this difference in frequency, we must consider what each class consists of, and how each category of word is used.

3.1.1 Open Word Classes

The most familiar parts of speech probably belong to the four open word-classes, or major parts of speech. As noted, these are the words that carry most meaning in English sentences, and they are listed below. They are described in terms of their *meaning, form and function* (although the *function* of these words will be considered in more detail in Chapter 4 when we look at phrases). Note that when using *abbreviations*, we use CAPITALS for the initial letter of a major part of speech and lower-case letters for the minor ones. The letters in brackets are the usual abbreviations.

noun (N)

These are traditionally described as 'naming words'. They refer to objects of all kinds, from observable things in the real world (*cat, computer)* to philosophical abstractions (*beauty*).

Some nouns can be recognised by certain affixes such as <ness> in *kindness, goodness, thoughtfulness,* or <ion> in *generation, consideration, amalgamation,* etc. Nouns tend to have two forms, a singular and a plural. The regular plural is made by adding <s/es> to the singular noun, as in *dog/dogs, gas/gases.*

Nouns function as the headword, that is, the most important word, in noun phrases (e.g. *the fat canary*), but they can also modify other nouns or even adjectives (e.g. *canary yellow*). ·

verb (V)

These are traditionally described as 'doing words'. They designate activities of all kinds, and states of being.

Verbs have a variety of different forms (e.g., *he rounds the bend, he is rounding the bend, he has rounded the bend).*

They function as the headword of verb phrases, although certain forms of the verb also pop up elsewhere in different guises (see further, Chapter 5.6).

adjective (Aj)

These are essentially descriptive words, which generally give us more information about nouns. They answer questions like 'How big is it?', 'What colour is it?' etc.

Unlike nouns, their form does not change (e.g. *fat* in *one fat cat, two fat cats*). Some adjectives can be identified by affixes such as <ful>, as in *beautiful, plentiful,* or <ive> as in *aggressive, responsive, attentive.*

They function as the headword in adjective phrases, or as modifiers in noun phrases (e.g. *utterly hopeless,* and *hopeless case).*

adverb (Av)

These words are also descriptive, but they are associated primarily with verbs. They give information like WHEN something was done (*yesterday),* or HOW (*sweetly)* or WHERE (*nowhere)* or TO WHAT EXTENT (*deeply).*

Like adjectives, their form does not change. Many of them can be identified by the Adverbial affix <ly>.

They can appear as the headword in Adverbial phrases (e.g. 'never' in *almost never)* but they can also modify adjectives (e.g. 'deeply' in *deeply sorry)* and other adverbs (e.g. 'almost' in *almost never).*

The four open-class items, nouns, verbs, adjectives and adverbs, in summary, express much of the meaning of any utterance or sentence. They can be distinguished by their form, function and meanings – but they share a capacity for being added to, as we find new things we need to express in our daily lives. The job of the much more frequent closed-class items is mainly to signal the relationship between the open-class items in any stretch of speech or writing, as we shall now see.

3.1.2 Closed Word Classes

There are seven closed word-classes or minor parts of speech. Grammarians vary in the terminology they use for these classes, so some alternative labels are given in brackets. Often these labels subdivide the main category. Remember, abbreviations for the closed word classes use lower-case letters, such as *(d)* and *(a).*

determiner (d)

Determiners are rather like adjectives in that they modify nouns in noun phrases. Unlike adjectives, however, they don't *describe* nouns – instead, they *specify* which noun it is, or who it belongs to, or which number in a sequence it is, or how much of it there is. Determiners include the following:

> *the* (definite article);
> *a* (indefinite article);
> *this, that, these, those* (demonstratives);
> *my, your, his, her, its, our, their* (possessive adjectives);
> *one, four, twenty, first, ninth, last,* etc. (enumerators, indicating definite quantities; note that some enumerators can also be nouns, e.g. 'Are you going to her *twenty-first?*');
> *some, any, no, all, many, most, whole,* etc. (indicating indefinite quantities).

If a phrase has both an adjective and a determiner, then the rule is that the determiner precedes the adjective in the noun phrase, as in

$$\text{his} \quad \text{old} \quad \text{bicycle}$$
$$\text{d} \quad \text{Aj} \quad \text{N}$$

Adjectives can be compared:

$$\text{big,} \quad \text{bigger,} \quad \text{biggest}$$
$$\text{Aj} \quad \text{Aj} \quad \text{Aj}$$

Determiners cannot:

$$\text{some,} \quad \text{*somer,} \quad \text{*somest.}$$
$$\text{d}$$

Broad Scots has a slightly different determiner system from English. In both speech and writing in Scots, we find further demonstratives:

2. **would cuiver maist o *thir* heids**
3. **that was all wood wool in *thae* boaxes**
4. **looking for *yon* thing**
5. **We got *thon* stuff for it**

Thir in older Broad Scots is equivalent to 'these'; however in the SCOTS corpus it is seldom used in this sense. In the corpus it is mostly used as a phonetic spelling of 'there/their'. However, on the few occasions when it is used as a demonstrative, it can mean 'these', as it does above. *Thae* or *they* are also Broad Scots equivalents of 'these'. The Scots demonstratives *yon/thon* are used to refer to things that are perceived to be at a distance: where 'this/these' refer to things that are close to the speaker, 'that/those' refer to things that are further away, and 'yon/thon' refer to things that are at an even greater distance. 'Yon/thon' have identical meanings, and each can be used to modify singular or plural nouns:

6. **It must be *yon* time**
7. **can I hae *thon* can o coke?**
8. ***Yon* jet-black een that ance burnt bricht**
9. **You can dee *thon* bonnie shapes, can't you?**

Many of the other determiners have English and Scots forms – *four* corresponds to *fower* for example, and *all* corresponds to *aw/aa/a'*, but the basic system is the same. That is, demonstratives apart, the determiner system of Scots and English is largely identical.

auxiliary verb (a)

Auxiliary verbs modify main verbs in verb phrases. To generalise, when we add an auxiliary verb to a main verb in a verb phrase, we alter the sense of *time reference, duration, possibility* or *obligation*. There are two types of auxiliary verb:

> *be, have, do*   (primary auxiliaries)
> *can, may, must, shall, would,* etc.   (modal auxiliaries)

The primary auxiliaries alter the sense of time reference and duration, e.g.

> *he hid*   (no auxiliary)
> *he was hiding*   (auxiliary *be*)
> *he has been hiding*   (auxiliary *have* + *be*)

The modal auxiliaries add the senses of possibility and obligation, e.g.

> *he could hide*   (auxiliary *can*)
> *he should hide*   (auxiliary *should*)

The auxiliary verb system is discussed in more detail in Chapter 9. In the meantime, it is worth noting that the distribution and use of the auxiliary verbs is different in Scottish English and Southern British English, particularly in informal speech. Scottish speakers tend to avoid certain modal auxiliaries, like *may,* preferring to use other modal auxiliaries (like *will*) in combination with an adverb like *maybe.* Compare:

10. **I cannot [...] predict what issues *may* arise in the future**
11. **I'll *maybe* gie they weans a bath**

pronoun (pn)

[Pronouns are used to replace nouns and thus avoid repetition], e.g:

12. Sometimes *people* have to admit that *they* cannot achieve what *they*
    N ⟵――――――――― pn ⟵――――――――― pn
    had hoped to achieve.

The pronoun *they* here replaces the noun *people.* There are different kinds of pronoun, and they can be subcategorised as follows:

I/me, you, he/him, she/her, it, we/us, they/them (personal pronouns)
mine, yours, his, hers, its, ours, theirs (possessive pronouns)
myself, yourself, etc. (reflexive pronouns)
someone, anyone, some, one, all, none, few, little, etc. (indefinite pronouns)
who, whom, whose, which, that (relative pronouns)
what? where? why?, etc. (interrogative pronouns)
this, that, these, those (demonstrative pronouns).

As with determiners, many of these pronouns have Broad Scots equivalents. For example, the personal pronoun *I* might be rendered *A* or *Ah,* or, if the speaker is from Dundee, *Eh.* In general, the spelling of pronouns in Scots is influenced by the pronunciation, e.g. *masel, yirsel* ('myself', 'yourself'), and so on.

Some Broad Scots pronoun forms are different in other ways. For example, the English possessive pronoun *mine* (example 13 below) is equivalent to *mines* in Broad Scots, probably because all the other possessive pronouns also end in *–s.* The alteration of an irregular grammatical feature to conform to a general pattern is a process known as 'analogy'. In (14) the 's' is added to *mine* to make it conform to *yours, his, hers, ours,* and *theirs.*

13. I would walk through living coal to take your hand in *mine.*
14. A took his haun in *mines*, and turnt it roon.

The interrogative pronouns in Scots are also rather different from those in English. In speech, many Scots use the interrogative pronoun *How?* as well as or instead of *Why?*

15. *Why* don't you go to the shops?
16. *How* do you no use that one?

In Scots, *Whit wey?* ('what way') is then used instead of *How?,* although, since *How?* and *Why?* are interchangeable in Scots, this means that *Whit wey?* can also mean *Why?*

17. ***Whit wey* can we git the pypar out?**
18. ***Whit wey* dae ye no ring yersel, dear?**

The demonstrative pronouns are similar in form to the demonstrative determiners. Instead of modifying a noun, the pronoun replaces it. Compare:

19. Can I borrow *this* book?   *this = determiner, book = noun*
20. Can I borrow *this*?   *this = pronoun*

The Scots determiners described earlier (i.e. *thir, thae/they, thon/yon*) can also be used alongside *this/these, that/those* as pronouns, e.g.

21. **Yeah I could easy understand *yon*, nae trouble wi *that*.**
                        pn   pn

Speakers of Broad Scots can evidently draw upon the Scots and English grammatical systems, and they frequently produce utterances that contain features of both.

preposition (pr)

The category of prepositions includes about fifty to a hundred little words that perform a wide range of uses in English and Scots. The ten most commonly used prepositions in English are *of, in, to, for, with, on, at, from, by* and *about.*

The term *pre-position* means 'position before a noun phrase.' Prepositions normally combine with nouns to form a wide variety of phrases, e.g.:

22. **they can sit *on* their old armchairs**
   pn a V **pr** d Aj   N

    and read *from* the pages *of* their weekly local paper
    c V **pr** d N **pr** d   Aj   Aj   N

Although prepositions combine with nouns, they do not modify them in the same way as adjectives and determiners do. Whilst adjectives are used to describe several of the nouns above *(old armchairs, weekly local paper)*, and determiners are used to identify the nouns *(their...armchairs, the pages,*

important

their...paper) a preposition gives a different kind of information, often about location, position or possession (*on...armchairs, from...pages, of...paper,* etc). Prepositions are therefore considered not to be modifiers in the noun phrase, but to combine with noun phrases to give prepositional phrases (see further, Chapter 5.4.5).

Different varieties of English and Scots prefer different prepositions in particular phrases. Consider, for example, which preposition you prefer to use in the following contexts:

23. **the situation for Gaelic is rather different ___ that of the other languages.**
24. **Did you find Aberdeen different _____ Glasgow?**
25. Morrissey is no different ____ any other pop star.

The choice of preposition to link the noun or pronoun to the adjective *different* depends partly on the context of the utterance and partly on the background of the speaker. In (23) the speaker used *to,* in (24) the speaker used *from* and in (25) the speaker used *than.* As the lack of bold highlighting indicates, the third example is not from the SCOTS corpus, which at the time of writing contains only one, barely audible, example of *different than,* in a recording of a young child from NE Scotland. Example (25) comes instead from the British National Corpus, where it is still a minority choice compared to *different from+ noun.* Peters (2004: 153) suggests that British speakers generally prefer *different from+noun* to *different to + noun* by a ratio 6 to 1, while American speakers seldom use *different to,* and are more likely to use *different than+noun.* Peters also points out that there are contexts in which most speakers of any kind of English will opt for *than,* as this example from the BNC also shows:

26. ethical statements do indeed do something more or different *than* merely state facts

Clearly, *merely state facts* is not a simple noun or noun phrase, so *than* has a different kind of linking function here. It is a conjunction, rather than a preposition, and it introduces a sequence of adverb (*merely*), verb (*state*) and noun (*facts*).

The distribution of prepositions varies not only across British and American English but across English and Broad Scots too. For example, there is variation in the use of preposition used to link *married/merrit* to the following noun phrase:

27. **his sister was married *to* a Black Douglas**

28. **The Duke of Kent is married *to* a lady**
29. **Thae sons merrit *oan* Moabite weemen**
30. **He was merrit *tae* a wife as daft as hissel**

conjunction (c)

Conjunctions link grammatical units (i.e. words, phrases or clauses) in different ways. Conjunctions include *and, but, or, if, that, where, when, although, because* and others.

As we shall see in more detail in Chapter 8, there is a distinction between *coordinating conjunctions* (i.e. *and, but, or*) and *subordinating conjunctions* (e.g. *if, that, where, when,* etc.). For the time being, we simply give an example of a coordinating conjunction and a subordinating one, using brackets to show the grammatical units that are being linked:

31. **[they want everything to be good], *but* [they don't think about what good is.]**
32. **[It was a grand day for the bairns too [*because* they got to roll eggs.]]**

As you can see from the examples, the coordinating conjunction *but* links two separate grammatical units, one on either side of the conjunction. In contrast, the subordinating conjunction *because* combines one grammatical unit with another by embedding it inside the main grammatical unit. Although the way that they function is rather different, it is the fact that *both types of conjunction link sequences of language* that allows us to put them in the same grammatical category.

interjection (i)

Interjections are used to attract attention, express emotion, etc. and include expressions like *hello, yes, oh, och, oh dear, ugh, tut tut,* etc. Proper names used to attract or draw attention are a special kind of interjection, often called a vocative, as in:

33. *John*, **do not get a desire for a motorbike**
    i

Until recently, interjections have been rather neglected by grammarians, for various reasons. Most obviously, until the advent of large-scale corpora that included information about speech as well as writing, it was difficult for grammarians to see how these apparent grunts and other noises were used in discourse. However, as corpora have become more widely used, it is clear that interjections are both frequent and meaningful. Carter and McCarthy (2006: 214-235) describe the use of various interjections in spoken English, including the use of such expressions as 'discourse markers' to indicate the beginning or the end of a speaker's turn or the topic being discussed. Example (34) represents part of a conversation from the SCOTS corpus, among several female speakers (F1054, F1005 and F1006) plus a solitary male (M1004). The speakers are discussing the words used for different concepts, but are interrupted by the noise of the washing machine that belongs to one of the participants:

34.   **F1054: *Ehm, well* speakin of [inaudible] *Oh!* Do you need to get that?**
     F1005: //[inaudible] machine, sorry, it's ma washin//
     F1006: //[laugh]//
     M1004: //She's not.//
     F1005: //[?]machine[/?].//
     M1004: She's a producer.
     F1005: Aye.
     F1054: *Anyway, ehm*, what about, speaking of attractive, what other words would you use for 'attractive' in the 'getting personal' section?

Here, we can see how interjections signal the introduction, shifting and resumption of topics. *Ehm, well* indicate a new topic is being introduced; *oh* indicates an unexpected interruption; and *anyway, ehm* indicates that an earlier topic is being re-introduced.

negative (n)

As the name suggests, this little grammatical particle is used to negate a verb. The way verbs are negated tends to differ in English and Scots. In written and spoken standard English, verbs are negated by placing *not* or *n't* after the auxiliary verb:

35. **I'm *not* going to change just to suit you.**
36. **I was*n't* going to buy three tickets to find out.**

At a glance, the Scottish system of negation seems to mirror the English one: *no* is used in place of *not* and *–nae* or one of its variants corresponds to *–n't*. Speakers can switch back and forth between the systems for dramatic reasons:

37. **I'm *no* goin back. I am *not* going back to that Sunday School.**
38. **she does*nae* go in for that either.**

However, there are differences in some details. In standard English, the contraction *-n't* is not used with the verb *am;* however, in Scots it is possible to use the contractions *-n't* and *-nae* with *am*. Compare:

39. **No, I'*m not* a plumber, no.**
40. **I kind of haven't been a bike nut and still *amn't.***
41. **No I *amnae.***

In English the restriction on the contraction of *am* and *–n't* affects the form used in tag questions with the first person pronoun. In English the anomalous tag *aren't I* is used:

42a. **I'm dead, *aren't* I?**

It would be possible for a Scottish English speaker to say:

42b. I'm dead, *amn't* I?

Alternatively, a Scottish English speaker might prefer:

43. **I'm a foster-mother to trade, *am I not*?**

In Broad Scots, the emphatic acknowledgement that might follow such a question could involve the use the verb *to be* as both an auxiliary and as a main verb (i.e. *am + are)*. This, in turn, can be affirmed or negated:

44. Aye, I'*m ur.*
45. Naw, I'*m urnae.*

However, these negative uses are hard to capture, and so far they are not recorded in the SCOTS data.

3.2 Issues in Identifying Word Classes

The bulk of this Chapter has been taken up with identifying different categories of word in English and Scots. In the broad category of open-class words, or lexical items, we have focused on the four major word classes of *noun, adjective, verb* and *adverb*. In the broad category of closed-class words, or grammatical items, we have looked at the seven minor word classes of *determiner, auxiliary verb, pronoun, preposition, conjunction, interjection* and *negative*. When beginning grammatical analysis it is necessary to label the words you find in an utterance according to these categories.

However, this kind of categorisation is not always easy, for a number of reasons. As noted earlier, many word forms in English function as more than one part of speech. For example, you might have noticed that the word *round* occurs in all four of the major parts of speech. In fact, it occurs in five of our eleven word-classes in all:

46. **her fingernails are *round* at the top**	Aj
47. **it is smudged *round* the edges**	pr
48. **let's have a *round* of applause**	N
49. **He walked *round* and *round* and *round*, sneering**	Av
50. **they *rounded* the corner to the last distillery**	V

As ever, it is important to pay attention to meaning, function and form when classifying words.

3.3   Activities

3.3.1   Exploring Open Word Classes

1.   *Nouns* can be identified functionally in that they are the most important word in phrases that begin with 'a/the/this/that'. You can test this hypothesis by carrying out an Advanced Search in the SCOTS corpus for phrases that begin with *a + adjective*. (Instructions on how to do concordance searches are given in Section 2.3 above.) Try searching for 'a big' 'the awful', etc., and then identify the noun that acts as a headword in each phrase. Some concordance lines for 'this old' are given below. Identify the headword and check whether it meets all the criteria for 'nounness':

> **this old boy**
> **this old thing**
> **this old boat**
> **this old dog**
> **this old, old story**
> **this old Stone Age relic**

2.   Search the SCOTS corpus for words ending in *–ful* and *–ive*. As shown earlier, you can do this by entering **ive* or **ful* as your search item. Your results should have forms strongly associated with *adjectives*. Test whether they also have adjectival meanings (ie are they descriptive?) and functions (e.g do they precede nouns; do they follow adverbs? do they appear after the verb 'to be'?). Some examples of **ful* are given below. If they are not adjectives, what are they?

it seemed to be an awful skoosh
there's some people with beautiful voices
you had to be careful
a carful of world-famous Shediac lobsters
your cheerful smile
they were serious, careful, thoughtful
make the information more colourful
how did that disgraceful rumour spread?
one national document that is mindful of urban and rural issues

3.   *Verbs* are identifiable mainly because of their varied forms. The meanings of verb phrases are complex and fascinating, and are explored in some detail in Chapter 9. To explore the verb phrase, search the SCOTS corpus for a regular verb, like *love,* but drop the final 'e' and add * to the end of it, to catch all the verb endings. How many of the examples are verbs? What kind of words modify verbs? Some results are given below for *lov**.

I *love* my Mummy sometimes
We would *love* to raise entry charges
Burns himself *loved* the dance
he *loves* making words up
Ah wis *lovin* yi

Some of the results of a SCOTS corpus search for *lov** show other kinds of words, e.g. *lovely,* an adjective, and *lover,* a noun. Interestingly, 'loving' appears several times, but as an adjective rather than as a verb, e.g. ***He talked with loving familiarity....*** The only comparable verb forms are found in Scots, in expressions such as ***Ah wis lovin yi.*** As we shall see in more detail later, with some exceptions English speakers tend to avoid using *–ing* forms of verbs that express mental or emotional activities. Scottish speakers are less likely to avoid these forms. A Scottish speaker is therefore more likely than an English speaker to say ***He was believing me, I could see,*** rather than *He believed me, I could see.*

4.   Many, but by no means all, *adverbs* end in *–ly.* Moreover, not all words that end in *–ly* are adverbs: we have just noted that *lovely* is an adjective, for example. Adverbs often fall into pairs with adjectives – *quick/quickly, slow/slowly, brave/bravely,* and so on. One way of exploring the difference between these word classes is to compare their uses in the SCOTS corpus. What other parts of speech are the adjective

awkward and the adverb *awkwardly* describing in the following examples?

there is an *awkward* silence
to defend the minister from *awkward* questions
a tufty at each end for getting into *awkward* corners

everyone is looking at them *awkwardly*
we were drinking the stuff *awkwardly* at the table
the other solicitor grappling *awkwardly* with an armful of files

5.   *Multiple Membership*

Many words can appear in more than one word-class – they have multiple membership. The way we assign these words changes according to their use in different sentences.   It is therefore important to pay attention to the meaning, form and function of words as they appear in different contexts.   In Chapter 2 we noted that *baby* can be a noun or a verb. Similarly, we saw above in examples 46-50 that *round* might appear as an example in several word classes. Can you classify *round* in the following examples?

a.   She had *round* blue eyes.
b.   Do you fancy a *round* of golf?
c.   The bus *rounded* the corner.
d.   Most soup-plates are *round*.

3.3.2 Identifying Words in Context

Parsing begins with the identification of words in written sentences or spoken utterances. In each of the two passages from the SCOTS corpus given below, assign the items in **bold** to the appropriate category of word.

Open-class items: **N, Aj, Av, V**   Closed-class items: **d, a, pn, pr, c, i, n**

Extract A: Christian Kay interviews Ian Rankin
In this extract, one of the authors interviews the Edinburgh author Ian Rankin about translations of his work. The website referred to is that of the Bibliography of Scottish Literature in Translation (BOSLIT: http://boslit.nls.uk). The slashes // indicate where the speakers are talking simultaneously.

CK: Right. But [1] **nowadays** your work is very widely translated. If you look up the BOSLIT website, you find there are t- ninety-eight translations of your books in circulation. And I think you said that was twenty-seven

47

languages. Would you li- can you give us some idea of the [2] **spread** of languages?

IR: Ehm, [3] **well** one of the first was Welsh. //Erm//

CK: //Really? *[laugh]*//

IR: 'Knots and Crosses' was translated into Welsh. But I remember gettin, and I can't find it, but I did get a letter from the the, whoever was publishin it in Welsh, I know it exists cause it's in [4] **the** National Library in Edinburgh, [5] **although** I've never seen a copy. Ehm, they said, 'We're having problems havin all these Scottish names; we're gonna change them to Welsh names.'

CK: *[audience laugh] [laugh]*

IR: And so they had the streets of Edinburgh teeming with Bronwyns and Dais,

CK: *[audience laugh] //[laugh]//*

IR: //erm which I thought was rather [6] **odd**.// Er, but it doesn't seem to be odd to people who translate books. Do you know, [7] **in** America they very blithely for years [8] **would** change 'pavement' to 'sidewalk',

CK: Mmhm

IR: 'boot' of the car to 'trunk' of the car, even if the the person sayin the word was Scots and would never use that. Ehm and just the last book that I wrote, 'Fleshmarket Close'; they [9] **changed** that in American to 'Fleshmarket Alley',

CK: [Uh-huh] *[audience laugh]*

IR: ehm, a street that does [10] **n't** exist, because [11] **they** felt that no American would know what a close was. Ehm so, I mean, the problems with translation aren't just in in other languages; they're actually in English as well.

Extract B: Letter to Canada

In this slightly edited text, a mother writes a letter to her daughter, who has recently taken up a university position in Canada. Again, identify the 11 word classes.

It was lovely to have an excuse for a chat on the Telephone on Saturday - and then we got your letter on Monday so now feel we are [1] **well** up to date with the news. I hope the house/flat hunting is going well. There would probably be more of a community feeling [2] **around** the Osborne Village area and a house or condominium apartment would suit you. I expect the apartments would be less anonymous and impersonal than the huge rented block you are in and you would probably find [3] **congenial** neighbours. However, [4] **we** will hear further from you. Are you alright money wise?

I hope the new office is now in order and that you are settling in to your new [5] **commitments**. Perhaps they are [6] **not** quite so new just 'official' now -

you've probably been doing most of the work already. I was surprised to read that it was 'Annabelle's last day' - has she left, or just gone off on holiday, [7] **or** just moved to another department? You will miss working with her but hopefully [8] **your** new colleague Beryl will prove as friendly and compatible!

I hope you enjoyed 'Cats'. Was it a professional touring company eg. the same company who [9] **performed** in Toronto? or was it just a co-incidence that it was on in both cities? Also the Folk Festival [10] **should** be fun. Did you wear your kilt? Too hot perhaps. Though I remember someone trying to insist that the woollen kilts worn by the Scottish soldiers in the desert kept out the heat!! Wishful thinking I imagine.

[11] **Well**, no more now.

Chapter 4   More about Words

4.0   About this Chapter

Chapter 3 introduced the eleven main types of word found in English and Scots, and distinguished between those that carry most of the meaning (open class words, or 'lexical items') and those whose function is mainly to modify the meanings of the lexical items and to signal the relationship between them (closed class words, or 'grammatical items'). Open-class items are subject to innovation as new words are introduced to the language; closed-class items tend to be a finite set, less subject to addition and change. We can easily think of a new noun or verb, for example, but language users are less likely to accept a new pronoun or a new auxiliary verb. In this Chapter we look further at the category of open-class words, in particular nouns, adjectives and adverbs. We touch here upon the subject of verbs, but this topic is so substantial that we return to it in more detail in Chapter 9.

4.1   More about Nouns

The most numerous class of words in the language is that of nouns. We use nouns to refer to items in the world, whether that world is real or imaginary. Nouns can be subdivided into smaller categories, using a range of criteria which are summarised below.

4.1.1   Abstract and Concrete

The traditional definition of a noun is that it is a 'naming word' which identifies a person, animal, place or thing. The type of noun that most clearly

51

performs this function is a *concrete noun*. These are words like *girl, student, chair, blackboard* which have obvious referents (*referent* = 'thing referred to') in the world around us. In all these cases we could point to the person or object referred to – and we often do if we are teaching a beginner the language. It is more difficult to do this with *abstract nouns*. We may know perfectly well what *Tuesday* or *happiness* or *philosophy* means, but we can hardly point to definite examples of them.

The distinction between abstract and concrete nouns is a traditional one, and it is clearly based on the meanings of the words. One question to ask is whether this distinction in meaning has consequences in the grammatical behaviour of abstract and concrete nouns – that is, do we use them differently in sentences, or combine them with different kinds of word? The answer is technically no; however, there is a tendency for abstract and concrete nouns to coincide with another kind of categorisation, one that *does* have an impact on the behaviour of nouns. That is, many abstract nouns are also mass nouns, while many concrete nouns are also count nouns. Certain determiners can modify mass nouns, while other determiners modify count nouns – so the distinction is more useful to grammarians.

4.1.2   Count, Mass and Collective Nouns

As noted in the introductory Chapter, we can divide nouns into (i) individual items that can be counted, e.g. *loaf/loaves*, (ii) substances which we tend to regard as indivisible wholes, e.g. *bread* and (iii) unitary bodies made up of a collection of individuals, e.g. *a team*. *Count nouns* refer to individual items which can be counted. *Mass nouns* refer to wholes (for example, we tend not to count **one, two or three breads*), and *collective nouns* refer to unitary bodies made up of a collection of individual items. Since they can be counted (e.g. *one, two or three teams*), collective nouns can be thought of as a special case of count noun. As we saw at the end of Chapter 1, they are special because often people use a plural verb with the singular noun (*the team is/are*), reflecting that the meaning of the noun expresses plurality, even if it is singular in form.

The interesting thing about count and mass nouns is that they often behave differently, that is they combine with other words in systematically different ways. Both mass and count nouns can occur after the definite article (*the*), but *only* count nouns occur as headwords after indefinite articles (*a, an*) or occur as plurals. Consider the following examples from the SCOTS corpus:

If we take a concrete count noun like *dish* we find that it occurs in a range of contexts. First, it occurs as the main word or 'headword' following the determiners *the* and *a*:

1. **the *dish* will be a failure**
2. **the metal lid covering the *dish***
3. **the *dish* she loved**

4. **a *dish* to look forward to**
5. **in a *dish* in the oven**
6. **a *dish* best served cold**

Secondly, we find the term in the plural form, *dishes,* e.g.:

7. **sinkful of dirty *dishes***
8. **6 butter *dishes***

Dish, then, fulfils all the criteria required of a count noun. It can be contrasted with a noun referring to a substance, like *milk. Milk* also appears as a headword after *the:*

9. **showing signs of having finished the *milk***
10. **the *milk* left in the bowl**
11. **the *milk* was boiled**
12. **they dissolve intae the *milk***
13. **he wid steal the *milk***

However, if you search the SCOTS corpus for *a milk* you will find only a few examples, and none of them is a headword. In all the SCOTS examples, *milk* modifies another noun that acts as the headword, e.g.

14. **a *milk* dish**
15. **a *milk* pudding**
16. **a *milk* and honey land**

A milk does not occur by itself, and there are no examples of the plural noun **milks*. Although *dish* and *milk* are both nouns, then, their different grammatical behaviour leads us to classify them as different kinds of noun, one a count noun and the other a mass noun.

Fewer/less, many/much and monie/muckle
In general, count and mass nouns differ in that each combines with different determiners. Look at the following data from the SCOTS corpus. Consider whether the nouns are mass nouns or count nouns. Then work out the grammatical rules for choosing the determiners *fewer/less* and *many/much:*

17. **It makes less noise**
18. **there seem to be fewer words**
19. **fewer and fewer teachers**

20. **many quaint sayings**
21. **many different cultural backgrounds**
22. **producing much coal**
23. **much furniture**

Technically, *fewer* and *many* should only occur with count nouns, and *less* and *much* should appear with mass nouns, as in the examples above. However, if we consider example (24), there is evidence that *less* is gradually encroaching into countable contexts associated with *fewer:*

24. **Fox destruction clubs generally use less dogs...**

At first glance, the Scots determiners *monie/muckle* appear to be parallel to *many/much,* that is we might assume that *monie* would be used with count nouns and *muckle* with mass nouns. However, the SCOTS corpus suggests that this distinction is not so clear-cut. Unlike *much, muckle* can be used as an Adjective, meaning something like *great* or *big*. In this sense, it can appear with count nouns, e.g.:

25. **these great muckle trees**
26. **a muckle pond**
27. **twa muckle message bags**

This seems to be by far the most common use of *muckle* in the corpus. However, *muckle* can also be used as a determiner, with a similar sense to *much,* and in these instances its use is limited to mass nouns:

28. **nae muckle wunner**
29. **naethin o muckle eese** [= nothing of much use]

Monie, like *many*, combines with countable nouns:

30. **monie times**
31. **monie helpins**
32. **monie fowk**

It might appear that a grammatical distinction such as count/mass noun is clear-cut and absolute. After all, we should be able to count things or not. However, as in many issues to do with grammar, there are interesting grey areas. The grammatical behaviour of some nouns – and their countability –

depends on how we think about them from utterance to utterance. Consider the following examples of those nouns that we can think about either as count nouns or as mass nouns, depending on their meaning in context:

33. **She arrives for** *coffee* **at ten-thirty** (the substance: mass noun)
34. **He hands them their** *coffees* (individual cups of coffee: count noun)
35. **I'm quite obsessive about** *chocolate* (the substance: mass noun**)**
36. **her grandmother loved good** *chocolates* (individual items: count noun)

As noted briefly above, collective nouns are an ambiguous little subgroup of count nouns that occur after both kinds of determiner, *a* and *the*. They are different because they can take either a singular or a plural verb, depending on whether we think of them as expressing a collection of individuals, an indivisible unit or a generalised concept. Collective nouns mainly refer to groups of people, animals, or things, e.g. *team, family, committee, staff, herd, flock*. The SCOTS corpus gives instances of when we use the words as singular units and as plurals:

37. **the team** *is* **magic** (individual unit: singular)
38. **his team** *are* **actively involved in their local community**
    (many individuals: plural)
39. **the family** *is* **the very basis on which society stands**
    (general concept: singular)
40. **I know John and Doll's family** *are* **well**
    (many individuals: plural)

As noted earlier, there is a general difference between North American and British conventions in relation to collective nouns: while North American educated usage tends to consider them as singular (and so Americans generally would say and write *the team is*), educated British speakers and writers now tend to consider them as plural (and so would say and write *the team are*).

4.1.3 Proper and Common Nouns

Another way of classifying nouns is into proper and common nouns. *Proper nouns*, such as *James* or *Glasgow*, refer to particular individuals. *Common nouns*, such as *man* or *village*, denote classes of items that are grouped together because of their shared characteristics. For example, the common noun *village* refers to the class of items sharing the general characteristic of 'small group of houses or homesteads clustered together'.

Proper and common nouns are also distinguished grammatically. Normally, only common nouns are modified by determiners:

41. **Are you *a plumber* then?**
       d   N

42. *Are you *a Fred* then?
        d N

43. ***The plumber* went and broke the sink.**
    d   N

44. * *The Fred* went and broke the sink.
      d   N

Because they refer to unique items, proper nouns tend not to be found in the plural:

45. **They sent twa *plumbers* tae the hoose.**

46. * They sent twa *Freds* tae the hoose.

It is, of course, possible to find some contexts in which it is acceptable to use proper nouns either with determiners or in the plural. Sometimes proper names are used to refer to a class of individuals that share a similar set of characteristics, as in this example from the SCOTS corpus:

47. **My, you're still *a* smart wee *Bobby Dazzler.***

It is also possible to conceive of a situation that involves two or more people sharing the same proper name, as in the traditional tale of the 'four Marys', a version of which is found in the SCOTS collection of texts:

48. **The other *Marys* join them and they gather and sway.**

It is also possible for a proper noun to become a common noun. This happens with *eponymous* words, where, for example, the name of an inventor, producer or user is given to an object, as in *biro, cardigan* or *hoover* (the last of which was produced but not invented by William Henry Hoover of New Berlin, Ohio):

49. **curry stains *the hoover* missed**

The lesson to take from these observations is that grammatical rules are based on *tendencies,* not absolutely strict, black-and-white distinctions. We bend and shape grammatical categories according to our perceptions and communicative needs.

4.2 More about Adjectives

Adjectives generally modify nouns, or they can occur after verbs as headwords in their own right:

50. **a *beautiful* drive**
51. **it was *beautiful*, it was *lovely***

Adjectives can be divided into two major classes, non-gradable and gradable.

4.2.1 Non-gradable Adjectives

Non-gradable adjectives denote absolute qualities such as nationalities or biological characteristics. For example, people are either *male* or *female, alive* or *dead, Australian* or *not Australian,* etc. Because they have this 'either/or' quality, such adjectives often come in pairs where each word is the opposite or *antonym* of its partner. *True/false* and *married/single* are other examples.

Because they express qualities that are theoretically absolute, it should logically be odd to find non-gradable adjectives in expressions like *very dead* or *very alive.* Logically, you are either alive or you are not. However, as we shall see, such combinations are not impossible.

4.2.2 Gradable Adjectives

Non-gradable adjectives are few in number compared to gradable adjectives. The majority of adjectives are gradable; that is, they measure qualities on a scale of size, value, etc., such as *young/old, tall/short, good/bad, early/late.*

Young/old are the key points on their scale, but other points can be slotted into the scale. Your choice of word may vary according to your own position on the scale: if you are twenty, then everyone over thirty might seem 'old'! Context also affects our perception of the word – scales differ according to what we are referring to. Thus a 'tall child' would be shorter than a 'tall man', a 'tall hatstand' shorter than a 'tall tree', because the range of possible heights varies in each case. The same is true of adjectives denoting values: a 'good party' has quite different characteristics from a 'good talking-to'.

If two scales are in use at once, then apparently nonsensical sentences make perfectly good sense:

52. A small elephant is a large animal.
   d Aj   N   d Aj   N

Note that this does not hold true for non-gradable adjectives:

53. *A female doctor is a male person.
    d Aj   N   d Aj   N

Gradable adjectives and non-gradable adjectives differ in other kinds of behaviour. For example, gradable adjectives are much more likely to have *comparative* or *superlative* forms that intensify their meanings. If a gradable adjective is made up of one or two syllables, the comparative and superlative forms are usually formed by adding *–er, -est* to the root form. If the adjective has more than two syllables, we indicate comparative and superlative meanings by using the adverbs *more/less* and *most/least:*

54. **its *close* association with hell**
55. **the bubble got *closer***
56. **my *closest* friend**

57. **an *interesting* example**
58. **slightly *more interesting***
59. **the *most interesting* or amusing sentence**

Note that, again because they express absolutes rather than points on a scale, it is less probable that non-gradable adjectives will be found in comparative or superlative forms:

60. *more female

61. *less silent

Although it is less likely, it is not impossible – as we can see in expressions like *He was more dead than alive.*

Finally, gradable adjectives are more likely than non-gradable adjectives to be modified by *degree adverbs* such as *rather, so* and *very:*

62. **they can be *rather boisterous.***
63. **this is *rather important.***
64. **I was *rather apprehensive.***

65. it's *so ghastly.*
66. he's *so funny.*
67. I'm *so glad.*

68. *very fond* of a dram
69. my heart is sound and *very strong.*
70. Wee Andy's in Australia. *Very busy.*

Non-gradable adjectives are not so frequently modified by degree adverbs. However, like so many grammatical rules, these ones can be broken for dramatic or humorous effect. Often the meaning of the non-gradable adjective is changed by its use in combination with a degree adverb. For example:

71. **In moments like these the Lane became** *so alive* **and full of colour...**

72. **Stovies, that's** *very Scottish...*

In the first example, the Lane is not literally coming alive; rather, the writer is using the non-gradable adjective to mean something like 'lively' or 'vibrant'. In the second, the non-gradable adjective is not expressing an absolute national category, but rather it means, here, 'characteristic of Scotland'. It is therefore not impossible to use degree adverbs with non-gradable adjectives, but occurrences are rarer and the meanings are dramatic, humorous or non-literal.

4.3   More about Adverbs

Adverbs, like other word classes, can be sub-categorised according to how they behave in phrases and sentences. We consider four common kinds here: degree adverbs, circumstance adverbs, attitude adverbs and connective adverbs.

4.3.1   Degree Adverbs

We encountered degree adverbs in the previous section, particularly in combination with gradable adjectives. Degree adverbs occur in phrases and articulate how intense something is, or to what degree it happens. Degree adverbs are often used in speech to soften or emphasise what is being said. Examples include:

73. **Shetland dialect's** *very* **different itself, isn't it?**
74. **That would be** *pretty* **cool.**
75. **I'm doing** *so awfully* **well.**

76. **He became conspiratorial, *almost* chummy.**

Broad Scots examples of degree adverbs include:

77. **It hidnae been an *awfie* guid week for Geordie Jooks.**
78. **Bit it wis a *gey* thrawn cuddy, ye see.**

Although they are mainly used in combination with adjectives, degree adverbs can be found, particularly in informal speech, before nouns:

79. **Stovies, that's *very* Scottish. Mm, well maybe it's *very* Dundee.**
               Av   Aj   Av   N

Some might argue that the phrase *very Dundee* is ungrammatical, since it combines a degree adverb and a proper noun. However, combinations like this are common and easy to understand – here 'Dundee' is taken not as the city itself as a physical entity, but as shorthand for the characteristics of the city, with a meaning something like 'very typical of Dundee'.

4.3.2   Circumstance Adverbs

Degree adverbs are sometimes grouped along with other circumstance adverbs, that is adverbs that tell us more about the action of a verb. However, here we have separated them, since degree adverbs usually appear as modifiers in an adjective or noun phrase (*so* ageist, *very* Dundee) while other circumstance adverbs appear as the headword in their own phrases, e.g. (*so badly*). Circumstance adverbs can be further distinguished on the basis of the kinds of circumstantial meaning they add to an utterance or sentence. It is often possible to identify them by asking questions about a sentence or utterance:

QUESTION	ADVERB	TYPE OF CIRCUMSTANCE
How did he sing?	Badly	*Manner*
When did he leave?	Yesterday	*Time*
Where is she now?	Here	*Place*

4.3.3   Attitude Adverbs

Attitude adverbs tell us something about the speaker's opinion about the information communicated. They therefore often occur at or near the beginnings of sentences or utterances, to put the information in a kind of attitudinal 'frame'.

80. and *fortunately* it was quite an easy birth, you know

How adverbs are sub-classified depends, as ever, on how they are used in any particular case. *Hopefully* and *sadly,* for example, could be grouped with circumstance adverbs of manner (how did someone do something?) rather than as attitude adverbs (how does the speaker feel about what he or she is saying?) You can explore the SCOTS corpus to determine which uses are more frequent. Can you distinguish the attitude adverbs from the circumstantial adverbs of manner in the following examples?

81. *Hopefully*, this will tidy up this side of Gibson Street.
82. *Sadly*, he is dealing with the bereavement of a close personal friend.
83. I waited *hopefully* for better things.
84. Morag raises the sword *sadly*.

4.3.4   Connective Adverbs

Connective adverbs form a link between units in a piece of discourse, such as sentences. Common ones include *however, so, therefore, yet, too, also,* and adverbs indicating a position in a sequence, such as *firstly, secondly, finally*. The meanings of connective adverbs tell us the relationship between the units of discourse that are being linked. In example (85), *therefore* tells us that a result, effect or conclusion is being linked to its cause; while in example (86) *however* links a piece of information with another piece that qualifies or counters it:

85. I bow to my colleagues here, who are practising teachers and

CAUSE

therefore know what is happening on the ground on any particular day.

+ EFFECT

86. Scots can perhaps be regarded as having reached its zenith as a recognised national language suitable for every purpose of life about the time of the Reformation in 1560.

STATEMENT

However, the process of evolution into a language distinct from English was arrested in the middle of the century by the introduction of an English translation of the bible by the reformers from Geneva.

+ QUALIFICATION

Since connective adverbs have a linking function, they are often confused with conjunctions, the closed-class set of words that link together grammatical units. Adverbs can often occupy different positions within a sentence, a feature which distinguishes them from conjunctions. Compare the following sentences:

87. **We were supposed to collect skis; *however*, the boots hadn't arrived.**
88. We were supposed to collect skis, *but* the boots hadn't arrived.

The words *however* and *but* both connect the two parts of the sentences, but they are still grammatically different – the first is an adverb while the second is a conjunction. Consequently, they are governed by different rules, or constraints (note also the different punctuation in each case). For example, the word *however* can be moved in the first sentence:

87a. We were supposed to collect skis; the boots, *however*, hadn't arrived.
87b. We were supposed to collect skis; the boots hadn't arrived, *however*.

The word *but* cannot move in the same way:

88a. *We were supposed to collect skis; the boots *but* hadn't arrived.
88b. *We were supposed to collect skis; the boots hadn't arrived, *but*.

If the last of these examples sounds like a plausible sentence, it is because in some varieties of spoken language in Scotland, *but* can be placed at the end of an utterance to mark the end of a speaker's turn:

89. **Big fur his age, but.**
i

Here it is not, however, working as a connective adverb but as an *interjection* that signals that the speaker has made his or her point and so invites the listener now to contribute to the dialogue.

4.4   More about Verbs

Verbs have many fascinating characteristics, some of which are dealt with more fully in Chapter 9 of this book. For the time being, it is sufficient to note some basic facts. First of all, there are two types of verb: open-class main verbs (V), and closed-class auxiliary verbs (a). The open-class main verbs carry the main meaning in the verb phrase, and these verbs appear in two forms, present and past.

90. **'My wife's name was Fiona,' I *say*.** (present tense form)

                                V

91. **'Aye,' *said* Willie, fair delighted.** (past tense form)

       V

In addition, the main verb can optionally combine with one or more auxiliary verbs which add certain types of meaning to the main verb. For example, auxiliary verbs can add nuances of time reference and duration, or express concepts such as whether something is hypothetical or fact, degree of certainty, or obligation:

92. **I *did say* I didn't give a damn about Joe.** (emphatic past tense)

     a   V

93. **I *would* just *say* 'bilin' if it was a personal thing.**

       a   V   (modal: habitual past event)

94. **It's disgusting, I *must say*.** (modal: obligation)

                a   V

There are Broad Scots versions of several of the modal auxiliaries, e.g.:

95. **Thrawn, some *micht say*.** (modal: possibility)

              a   V

96. **The're sumthin Ah *maun say* tae ye.** (modal: obligation)

               a   V

However, as noted earlier, the differences between Scots and English modal usage go beyond differences in form. Scottish speakers often prefer different ways of expressing concepts like possibility and obligation, and sometimes avoid particular modal auxiliary uses favoured south of the border.

These issues are dealt with more fully later. In the meantime, it is important simply to note that all standard written sentences should include a verb phrase, and that this phrase can be made up of a main verb on its own, or a main verb in combination with one or more auxiliary verbs, e.g.:

97. **I am fascinated by what you *have been saying*.**

                           a   a   V

4.5   Activities

These practice activities are intended to help you to review and understand the information in the preceding chapters, and to test your progress in acquiring the skills taught in this book. In general, the skills you are learning involve:

(1)   the accurate classification of words, phrases, clauses and sentences, using appropriate technical terms. Much of the first section of this book is taken up with developing a common technical vocabulary.

(2)   the accurate description of the relationship *between* words, phrases, clauses and sentences.

These classificatory and descriptive skills are essential for the exploration of corpora such as the SCOTS corpus. We need a common descriptive framework in order to develop more sophisticated accounts of how communication in English and Scots works.

Activity 1
Label the *open-class* parts of speech in the following passage from Sheila Mackay's *Mountain Music,* an extract from which can be found in the SCOTS corpus. Think about the reasons behind your decisions – i.e. are you relying on meaning, form or function, or a combination of the three? For convenience, sections of the passage are numbered.

(1) We blethered in French, our only common language.
(2) He spoke of an arduous journey, many months long, over deserts, dusty roads and the sea itself,
(3) to get to Palma where he lives now in a barrio with other Sengali men.
(4) Later, I bought UV sunglasses from an older man
(5) who told me he had a wife and several children back home
(6) and that it would be one year and one month before he could go back.
(7) He was counting the days.

Look at the closed-class words in the passage. What can you say about their role in the text compared to the open-class items?

Activity 2
From the <u>underlined</u> words in the passage, select examples of the following:
(a) a count noun **(b)** a gradable adjective **(c)** a comparative adjective **(d)** a non-gradable adjective **(e)** a possessive determiner **(f)** an adverb of time **(g)** a preposition **(h)** a conjunction **(i)** a main verb **(j)** a modal auxiliary verb **(k)** a pronoun

We <u>blethered</u> in French, <u>our</u> only common language. He spoke of an arduous <u>journey</u>, many months long, <u>over</u> deserts, <u>dusty</u> roads and the sea itself, to get to Palma where he lives now in a barrio with other <u>Sengali</u> men. <u>Later</u>, I bought UV sunglasses from an <u>older</u> man who told <u>me</u> he had a wife and several children back home <u>and</u> that it <u>would</u> be one year and one month before he could go back. He was counting the days.

Activity 3
Give your own examples of the following:

a) an open word-class item   f) a pronoun
b) a closed word-class item   g) a mass noun
c) a circumstance adverb of manner h) a non-gradable adjective
d) a connective adverb   i) a determiner
e) a preposition   j) a modal auxiliary verb

Take a sample of two open and two closed parts of speech from the examples you have given and search the SCOTS corpus for them. Do your findings support your classifications?

Activity 4
Label the underlined parts of speech in the following paragraph, also from Sheila Mackay's *Mountain Music*. Sort the items into open and closed parts of speech.

At a <u>cornucopic</u> vegetable stall, an ebullient young Mallorcan
<u>offers</u> me a Spanish lesson:
'*Espinacas.*' Holding up a <u>bundle</u> of dewy green leaves.
'*Medio kilo, por favor.*'
<u>Then</u> a bunch of plump green beans:
'*Judias verdes,*' he smiles <u>as</u> I repeat: 'Hoodias berdee'.
The lesson continues, my basket fills, and <u>so</u> pleased is he <u>with</u>
our joint effort that <u>he</u> throws in extra mandarins as <u>a</u> reward.

Activity 5
Label ALL the parts of speech in the first sentence of the above extract by writing the abbreviation under each item, e.g.

Jack ran into the room.
N   V   pr   d   N

At a cornucopic vegetable stall, an ebullient young Mallorcan offers me a Spanish lesson.

Activity 6
We noted in 4.2 and 4.3 that degree adverbs tend to be used with gradable adjectives, e.g. *very kind.* One degree adverb *is* used with both gradable and non-gradable adjectives. Look at the following examples and explain what the degree adverb *quite* means when it is followed (a) by a gradable adjective and (b) by a non-gradable adjective:

i)   **Her long face seemed *quite kind.***
ii)   **[their] parents are *quite anxious***
iii)   **That option was *quite attractive.***

iv)   **[we] were *quite appalled***
v)   **your father's efforts on her behalf were *quite astonishing***
vi)   **She watches it burn thoughtfully. When it is *quite burnt* she bursts into tears.**

It is evident from the examples above that *quite* has two very different meanings: when it precedes a gradable adjective it can be substituted by another adverb like *fairly,* e.g. *fairly attractive;* but when it precedes a non-gradable adjective it can be substituted by an adverb like *completely,* e.g. *completely burnt.* Depending on whether you understand *anxious* as a gradable or an absolute state, *quite anxious* can either mean *fairly anxious* or *completely anxious.* In spoken English, this ambiguity would be resolved by stress and intonation – how would you pronounce the phrase to express the two different senses?

As the example of *anxious* shows, it is not immediately clear whether adjectives are inherently gradable or non-gradable. Look at the selected examples from concordance lines that include the degree adverb *very* followed by an adjective. Try to sort the adjectives into gradable and non-gradable adjectives. In the case of the non-gradable adjectives, explain why the combination with a degree adverb is appropriate:

i)   **it was *very brave* of you**
ii)   **it wisnae *very big***
iii)   **[his eyes] were exceptionally powerful and penetrating, *very black***
iv)   **a school essay written by a *very bright* pupil**
v)   **we were *very conscious* of that**
vi)   **I get *very cross* and kick her**
vii)   **You are, I can tell, a *very private* person**

It will be evident from the above that, as with count and mass nouns, the difference between gradable and non-gradable adjectives can be a matter of perception that varies from context to context. In example (v), you might argue that *conscious,* for example, should express an absolute state – you are either conscious or unconscious – and therefore it should be a non-gradable adjective. However, it is often used, as above, as a synonym for *aware,* which is more of a scalar attribute, and so gradable. Therefore, we can use *conscious* as a gradable adjective when we mean something like *aware,* and as a non-gradable adjective when we mean the opposite of *unconscious.* Other unusual uses in the above examples are *very black* (iii) and *very private* (vii), where the absolute, non-gradable adjectives are being further intensified.

Now that you have reached the end of this Chapter, you should be confident in identifying different kinds of word. We now go on to consider one of the most important topics in grammar: how words cluster into phrases.

Chapter 5   Combining Words Into Phrases

5.0 About this Chapter
5.1 Phrases
5.2 Headwords
5.3 Modifiers
5.4 Types of Phrase
5.4.1 Noun Phrases (NP)
5.4.2 Verb Phrases (VP)
5.4.3 Adjective Phrases (AjP)
5.4.4 Genitive Phrases (GP)
5.4.5 Prepositional Phrases (PP)
5.4.6 Adverb Phrases (AvP)
5.5 Adverbs and Prepositions
5.6 Participles: are they Verbs, Adjectives or Nouns?
5.7 Adjectives and Nouns as Modifiers
5.8 Activities

5.0   About this Chapter

So far we have looked mainly at words as individual grammatical constituents. In this Chapter, we begin to consider how words combine with each other. We look at how words are combined into phrases, as a first step towards combining them into larger grammatical structures, namely clauses and sentences. The Chapter defines phrases, considers the nature of their constituents (namely modifiers and headwords), outlines the different types of phrase, and concludes by considering some issues that sometimes make the analysis of phrases difficult.

5.1   Phrases

When we are doing grammatical analysis, we assume that a phrase consists of *one or more* words. As noted in passing earlier, this is an example of how grammatical terminology differs slightly from everyday usage, where 'phrase' usually means *two or more* words. In grammar, we assume that a phrase can consist of a single word, which can then be expanded or 'projected' into a phrase by the addition of certain other words, eg.

1. **coffee**   one-word phrase
2. **Turkish coffee**   two-word phrase
3. **sweet, Turkish coffee**   three-word phrase
4. **strong, sweet, Turkish coffee**   four-word phrase
   etc.

When parsing, we identify phrases by using *round brackets*. It is important to be consistent in this – square brackets and other kinds of bracket are used to signify other types of grammatical constituent. For each word in a phrase, we put an abbreviation below the line to indicate (a) the form of the phrase, and (b) the word-classes inside the phrase:

5.   (We)   (drank)   (coffee.)
  NP pn **VP** V **NP** N

6.   (The Russians)   (were drinking) (strong, sweet, Turkish coffee.)
  NP d N   **VP** a V   **NP** Aj Aj   Aj N

Sentence (6) is longer than sentence (5), but its structure is essentially the same. Both sentences contain three phrases each: two noun phrases (NPs) and one verb phrase (VP). The three phrases in Sentence (6) consist of more than one word. Think about the relationship between the words within each phrase of Sentence (6). We shall return to this topic below.

5.2   Headwords

The most important word in a phrase is the *headword* or *head* (H), which gives the phrase its name. For the purposes of analysis, we assume that each phrase has one (and only one) headword – although there are some grammarians who dispute this rule.

Thus in sentence (5) we have two Noun Phrases (NP), the first consisting of a single pronoun (pn) and the second of a single noun (N). They are linked by a Verb Phrase (VP) consisting of a single verb. Since each phrase consists of only one word, that word *must* be the headword, and is marked H above the line.

    H   H   H
5.   (We)   (drank) (coffee.)
  NP pn **VP** V **NP** N

In a multi-word phrase, we can identify the headword by means of a *subtraction test*, i.e. by stripping away words in order to see which words are essential to the structure of the sentence. By using subtraction, we can reduce *The Russians were drinking strong, sweet, Turkish coffee* to different sequences, e.g.:

6a. (Russians) (drinking) (coffee)

6b. (The) (were) (strong, sweet, Turkish)

Although not grammatically well-formed, the first example does communicate all the basic information in the sentence. The second example does not convey much information on its own. This tells us that the headwords are the nouns and the main verb, rather than the adjectives and the auxiliary verb. The adjectives and the auxiliary verb *modify* the headwords. Therefore, a fuller analysis of the sentence is:

```
     M   H             M   H            M      M      M    H
6.  (The Russians)  (were drinking)  (strong, sweet, Turkish coffee.)
    NP  d   N        VP  a   V        NP  Aj    Aj     Aj   N
```

This may look like a complicated diagram, but take a few seconds to examine it systematically.

i)   The three phrases are shown in round brackets.
ii)   We give each phrase a phrase label below, e.g. NP, VP.
iii)   We give each individual word a word label below, e.g. d, N, a, V.
iv)   We show how each individual word relates to the others in each phrase by labelling each word as a modifier (M) or a headword (H).

Steps (iii) and (iv) in this process tell us respectively the *form* of each word (i.e. the class to which it belongs), and its *function* (i.e. whether or not it modifies the other words in the phrase).

5.3   Modifiers

Words like adjectives ('strong, sweet, Turkish') and auxiliary verbs ('were') function as modifiers in the phrase. That is, they give us extra information about the headword, usually by narrowing down its meaning to make it more specific.

Theoretically, there is no limit to the number of modifiers we can add to a phrase, but the presence of too many can be aesthetically unpleasing, or difficult for the mind to process. From the SCOTS corpus concordance for the word 'incredible', for example, we find uses of the adjective as the sole modifier in a noun phrase:

7. **incredible hands**

We also find the adjective as part of a much longer noun phrase:

8. **the most incredible littoral explosions**

Note that determiners, like adjectives, function as modifiers. In the second NP, 'the' has a specifying function, indicating to the reader, in this case, that the identity of the set of explosions in question can be recovered from the text itself – the sentence goes on to relate that they were in fact 'on a flow south of here'.

Many word-forms in English can be both nouns and adjectives. A concordance search for the word 'yellow', for example, gives both adjective uses and noun uses, as we see in these examples of a parent talking to a young child:

9. **See, you're putting** *the yellow pen* **onto the blue.**
10. **I think you've mixed some o** *the yellow* **and some o the red into that white.**

In (9) the words *the* and *yellow* modify the noun *pen*. The phrase is therefore classified as a Noun Phrase (NP), and the modifier *yellow* is an adjective.

In (10) the word *yellow* is the headword, and it is modified by the determiner *the*. The phrase is therefore clearly a Noun Phrase – but how do we classify the headword? Either we can say that it is an adjective acting as the headword of a Noun Phrase, or we can re-classify the word in this context as a noun. Our dilemma may be represented thus:

	M	H
10a.	**the**	**yellow**
	d	Aj/N?

There are various arguments for adopting either approach; however, for the purposes of this book we shall adopt the latter approach, and argue that if a word *functions* as a noun (e.g. if it is a headword modified by a determiner) then it *is* a noun. In the tasks in the previous section, we saw similar issues with the adjectives *French* and *Mallorcan,* which can also function as the headwords of Noun Phrases, e.g.

11. **I tried** *my French* **out on the oldest member.**

Here, we can argue that *French* is effectively a noun. It is the headword of a NP, it is modified by a determiner *my,* and it could be used alongside an adjective, e.g. *my poor French*. In many ways, then, it passes the test of 'nounness', even though formally it looks like an adjective.

5.4 Types of Phrases

So far, then, we have established that phrases are generally made up of a headword with an optional and variable number of modifiers. We can even classify a word by looking at whether it is functioning as a headword or modifier, and how it interacts with other words in the phrase. We now turn to the main types of phrase in more detail.

There are six types of phrase in the system of grammar described in this book:

Noun Phrase (NP)	Verb Phrase (VP)
Adjective Phrase (AjP)	Genitive Phrase (GP)
Adverb Phrase (AvP)	Prepositional Phrase (PP)

In the examples below, we shall focus on each phrase in turn, showing each in the context of a sentence. We analyse each of the other phrases in the sentence for future reference; however, at a first reading you should pay particular attention to the form and function labels that are in **bold**.

5.4.1 Noun Phrases (NP)

The headword in a NP is usually either a noun or a pronoun (for pronouns, see 3.1.2 above). Occasionally, as we have just seen, the headword can be a word otherwise used as an adjective, as in *the yellow* above. There are two NPs in the following sentence:

```
        H     M   H      M   M   H
12.   (This) (should be)  (a happy day)
      NP pn  VP a  V     NP d  Aj  N
```

A NP can contain one or more modifiers; these are usually determiners, adjectives or nouns other than the headword, as in:

```
      M       M        M    H
13.  (the international book festival)
     NP d     Aj       N    N
```

5.4.2 Verb Phrases (VP)

It is important to remember that the headword of a VP is always a verb. As we have seen, verbs are divided into the open-class MAIN VERBS (V), which carry most of the lexical meaning, e.g. *talk, run, love,* etc., and closed-class AUXILIARY VERBS (a), which modify the main verb. The main verb is always the headword. The PRIMARY AUXILIARIES (*be, have, do*) can be either main verbs or auxiliaries depending on whether they stand alone or modify other verbs. A search of the SCOTS corpus for *consider** results in, among other items, different forms of the verb (*consider, considers, considered, considering*) either standing alone or modified by different kinds of auxiliary verb, e.g.

		H	H	H			
14.		**(Consider)**	**(yourself)**	**(lucky.)**			
		VP V	NP pn	AjP Aj			

	H	M	H	H	M	H	H
15.	**(We)**	**(don't consider)**		**(it)**	**(a swearword)**		**(now.)**
	NP pn	**VP a**	V	NP pn	NP d	N	AvP Av

	H	M	H	M	H	x	H
16.	**(We)**	**(are considering)**		**(the petitions)**		**(before us.)**	
	NP pn	**VP a**	V	NP d	N	PP pr	pn

	M	H	M	H	M	H	
17.	**(Other areas)**		**(might consider)**	**(that approach.)**	
	NP d	N	**VP a**	V	NP d	N	

	H	M	H	M	M	H	H
18.	**(We)**	**(must consider)**		**(our next steps)**		**(soon.)**
	NP pn	**VP a**	V	NP d	Aj	N	AvP Av

5.4.3 Adjective Phrases (AjP)

The headword of an AjP is an adjective. Remember that adjectives can simply appear as modifiers in a NP, as in the first example below. But sometimes the adjective itself is modified, and so it becomes the headword of its own phrase, embedded inside the NP, as in the second example (and as we shall see in more detail later). AjPs are also treated as separate if the adjective is separated from the noun it modifies by a linking verb:

	H	M H	M	H			
19.	**(he)**	**('s got)**	**(incredible hands.)**			
	NP pn	VP a V	NP Aj	N			

	H	M H	M	M	M	H	M	H
20.	**(you)**	**(can see)**	**(the**	**(most incredible)**	littoral explosions.)
	NP pn	VP a	V NP d	**AjP Av**	**Aj**	Aj	N

74

```
        x     H     H      H
21.    Gosh, (that) ('s)  (incredible.)
        i    NP pn  VP V  AjP Aj
```

In the last of the three examples given above, *gosh* is an interjection, here labelled as an 'x'. We do not consider that interjections systematically combine with other words to form phrases, and so we do not enclose it in brackets or consider it to be either a headword or a modifier. We treat *golly gosh, oh gosh* and even *by gosh* as single interjections too.

5.4.4 Genitive Phrases (GP)

Genitive phrases indicate a range of relationships such as *possession,* and they are marked by the use of the apostrophe, as in *the boy's book* (singular) or *ladies' shoes* (plural). This curious way of marking possession in Present-Day English, which causes so much confusion, is a relic of the Old English grammatical system. A thousand years ago, English marked the relationships between words by adding certain grammatical signals called *inflexions* to them (see further Hough and Corbett, 2006). In OE, <es> was added to certain nouns to indicate possession. The <'s> in PDE is a survivor of this ancient system, in which the possessive form is labelled 'the genitive':

| Old English: | *stān* | genitive: | *stānes* |
| Present-Day English: | *stone* | genitive: | *stone's* |

It is difficult to treat this throwback to Old English grammar in a description of the modern language. In this book, we resolve the issue by treating words like *stone's* as a phrase that can usually be paraphrased by a Prepositional Phrase with *of,* as in *of the stone.* This alternative way of indicating possession in English is a later innovation, based on French grammar. The headword of a Genitive Phrase is the noun plus the apostrophe plus *s*; this complex headword can be modified in the same way as other NPs. The main difference is that a Genitive Phrase tends to be used *as a whole* to modify another noun, in a NP or a Prepositional Phrase. Examples of Genitive Phrases from the SCOTS corpus include:

```
        H     H    M   M     H           H
22.    (this) (is) ( a (children's) book)
        NP pn VP V NP d  GP     N         N
```

75

```
        M   H      H      x  M M       H          H
23.     (your name) (went) (in  (the  policeman's) book)
        NP  d    N   VP V  PP pr GP  d       N          N
```

There are some tricky issues that the analyses above gloss over. The main one is to do with the determiner that comes before the Genitive Phrase – does it properly relate to the headword of the GP or to the headword of the NP in which it is embedded? In the first example, this is quite easy to answer: we would not say *this is **a** book of a children.* In other words, the determiner, *a,* seems to relate to the headword *book,* not to *children's,* so we place it outside the GP, but inside the NP. The second example is more ambiguous, because we can quite happily rephrase this as *in **the** book of **the** policeman.* Consequently, it is unclear whether to situate the determiner *the* inside the GP or not. In this case, we might argue that we can replace *the policeman* with *his* to give *in his book,* and so the determiner is best analysed as part of the GP. Genitive Phrases can be further expanded, for example by adding adjectives that describe the headword. Compare:

```
        H      H     M    M M H        H
24.     (this) (is)  (a super (children's) book)  = the book is super
        NP  pn VP V  NP d    Aj  GP N       N
```

```
        H     H    M M M       H          H
25. (this) (is)  (a  (young children's) book)  = the children are young
    NP  pn VP V  NP d GP Aj       N          N
```

Examples (24) and (25) illustrate a general principle in the analysis of phrase structure, namely that we are interested in showing how words relate to each other within the phrase – how, for instance, do the adjectives *super* and *young* relate to the other words in their respective phrases? The bracketing is an attempt to make these relationships explicit.

5.4.5 Prepositional Phrases (PP)

Prepositional Phrases (PPs) are easy to identify because they always begin with a preposition. *Pre-position* literally means 'the position *before* a NP'. This is the position where most prepositions occur for the good reason that prepositions turn NPs into PPs. Many PPs give us extra information about the place or time of an action:

```
        x   M      M        H       M M H       H          H
26.     (By the fourteenth century) (the (king's) territories) (were)
        PP pr  d        d        N   NP d GP  N        N       VP V
```

76

```
              M       M     H
        (productive earthly paradises.)
   NP     Aj      Aj      N
```

Other PP's are used metaphorically. Below, 'love' is being conceptualised as some kind of space into which people fall.

```
         H      H       H       H      H      x   H
27.    (boy)  (meets)  (girl,)  (they)  (fall)  (in  love)
       NP N   VP V    NP N    NP pn  VP V    PP pr  N
```

The reason why we put an 'x' above the line for prepositions was touched upon earlier – prepositions, like interjections, function neither as headwords nor modifiers. Rather, prepositions like *by, in, on, over,* and so on, indicate the relationship between the words that follow them and the rest of the sentence. They are essentially grammatical signals that indicate how phrases relate to each other.

5.4.6 Adverb Phrases (AvP)

Adverb phrases have adverbs as headwords. An adverb phrase can be a single adverb, or it can consist of an adverb as headword, modified by another adverb. In general, Adverb Phrases give us extra information about such things as the time, place or manner of the action described by the verb.

```
         H        M       H                H
28.  (Britain)  (is over-reacting)  (hysterically.)          MANNER
     NP    N     VP a      V        AvP   Av
```

```
         H          M    H            H
29.  (Domestics)  (were paid)  (monthly.)                    TIME
     NP    N       VP a    V    AvP  Av
```

```
       x      H     H      H      M     H
30.  Well   (I)   (left)  (it)  (right there.)               PLACE
     i   NP pn VP V NP pn  AvP Av   Av
```

The meanings of AvP's have much in common with Prepositional Phrases, since they too often give us information about time, place or manner. For example, the AvP in the first two of the above examples could be rephrased as *Britain is over-reacting in a hysterical way; Domestics were paid by the month.*

Degree Adverbs

As we saw in 4.4.1, there is a subset of adverbs that act as modifiers within Adjective and Adverb Phrases, specifically to intensify or downplay the quality expressed by an adjective or the manner of an action expressed by an adverb. The modifiers are called degree adverbs, and they include *very, rather, quite, fairly, so, much, extremely, totally* and others. Note how they function in the following phrases:

```
         H        H       M    H      x   M   H
31.   (Fiona)  (looked)  (so beautiful)  (in her anger.)
      NP    N   VP   V   AjP Av   Aj    PP pr  d    N
```

```
         H    M   H        M       H
32.   (They) (are doing)  (extremely badly.)
      NP pn  VP a   V    AvP  Av      Av
```

It is clear from the spoken documents in the SCOTS corpus that certain degree adverbs are increasingly popular in the conversation of younger people, for instance when one speaker is agreeing emphatically with another, as in the following use of *totally:*

33.   **F812: //do you know what I mean?//**
         F813: //mmhm// totally

Totally is one of several adverbs that can be used by themselves to make an emphatic confirmation – others are *absolutely,* and *certainly.* As well as being the headword of an adverb phrase, these adverbs can, of course, intensify other adverbs, for example, in another conversation from the SCOTS data:

```
                                          M       H
34. it gave them then a chance to like chat about stuff (totally informally)
                                         AvP Av      Av
```

The range of emphatic uses of *totally* in conversational English seems to be extending, as in the following examples, taken from different SCOTS conversations:

35. **I *totally* didn't see your note this morning**
36. **she was *totally* kind of grumpy**

This kind of grammatical creativity is common in the language of younger people; it marks off each succeeding generation as a distinct social group.

5.5 Adverbs and Prepositions

As we saw above, the meanings of AvPs and PPs have much in common. The same is true of individual adverbs and prepositions, and we therefore often find the same form being used for both parts of speech. The golden rule for distinguishing them is that *a preposition is ALWAYS combined with another word*, usually a noun phrase or a pronoun. An adverb, by contrast, is an independent unit. Compare the different grammatical roles played by the word *inside* in examples (37) and (38) from the SCOTS corpus:

```
         H      H          H          H
37.    (he) (remains) (unchanged)  (inside)
      NP pn VP V       AjP Aj      AvP Av
```

```
        H    M   M    H          x    M   M    H
38.    (that) (could be concealed)  (inside the trouser leg)
      NP pn VP a     a     V       PP pr  d   N    N
```

5.6 Participles: are they Verbs, Adjectives or Nouns?

Participles are forms of the verb that function as part of verb phrases. The participle forms of regular verbs end in *-ing* and *-ed,* as in *walking,* and *walked.* Although these forms are called, respectively, the present and past participles, they actually require an auxiliary verb to indicate the tense in a full verb phrase, e.g. *is/was walking* and *has/had walked.*

As will be evident in examples (37) and (38) above, with respect to *unchanged* and *concealed,* participles often develop into either adjectives or nouns. The participle *changed* has clearly become an adjective that has in turn been negated as *unchanged.* After all, we do not have in English the verb *to unchange.*

The multi-functionality of participles can sometimes cause ambiguity and hence problems for grammatical analysis. Examples (39) and (40) from the SCOTS corpus illustrate the issue:

39. **their flesh is hidden**
40. **the deprivation is hidden by the area's relative wealth**

In each of these extracts, *hidden* is a participle. The question is whether it is functioning as part of a Verb Phrase or part of an Adjective Phrase. To answer this kind of question, we can apply some possible tests.

Test 1: Passive to Active Verb

If the participle in question is a verb, then we should be able to change the verb phrase from the active to the passive voice (see further, Chapter 9). In other words, in the examples above, we should be able plausibly to change X *is hidden* to *Y hides X*. We can do this easily with example (40), changing *the deprivation is hidden* to *the area's relative wealth hides the deprivation*. In the case of (40), then, it looks very much as if *hidden* is the main verb, and *is* is an auxiliary verb. However, it is less clear that we can rephrase example (39) as *something hides their flesh*. To consider this example further we can apply a second test.

Test 2: True Adjectives

True adjectives can appear in two positions:

(i) in ATTRIBUTIVE position before the noun that they modify, e.g.

	M	M	H
41.	**(The happy couple)**		
	NP d	Aj	N

or (ii) in PREDICATIVE position after the NP + linking verb:

	M	H	H	H
42.	**(The world)**	**(is)**	**(happy)**	
	NP d	N	VP V	AjP Aj

If they are gradable, adjectives can take comparative and superlative forms, and be modified by degree adverbs, e.g. *The happier/happiest couple; The very happy couple*. Finally, participles which have undergone conversion to adjectives can form compound adjectives, e.g. *good-looking, hard-boiled, shit-scared*.

If we look again at *The flesh is hidden,* we see that we can satisfy all the tests of adjective status for *hidden* in this context. We can, for example, rephrase this sentence as a phrase with the participle in attributive position (*the hidden flesh*) and we could turn the participle into a compound adjective (*the half-hidden flesh*). There is, then, a good case for considering *hidden* in example (39) as an adjective. Of course, these two examples are reasonably clear-cut. There will remain cases where each possible analysis of the participle, as verb or adjective, will remain as plausible as the other.

5.7 Adjectives and Nouns as modifiers

Grammatical tests can be applied to other cases where it might not be immediately obvious how to classify a word in a phrase. For example, in noun or adjective phrases, it is not always immediately clear whether a modifier is an adjective or a noun. In the SCOTS corpus the word *cream* modifies a number of nouns, including *blouse* and *cake*. We can apply the test for true adjectives above to decide in which instances *cream* should be considered an adjective and in which it should be considered a noun modifier:

43. **cream blouse** ⟶ *the blouse was cream, a very cream blouse*

44. **cream cake** ⟶ **the cake was cream, *a very cream cake*

For example (a), the rephrasing satisfies the adjective test, and so *cream* can be considered an adjective in this context. However, the rephrasing of (b) sounds odder, and so in this context *cream* is probably still best considered as a noun modifier.

5.8 Activities

In earlier chapters we were concerned mainly with the classification of individual words. In this Chapter, we have taken the next step towards a full grammatical analysis by considering how words relate to each other in phrases (i.e. their *function*).

Activity 1
Look at sentences (a) to (j) and follow the steps given below:

1. Identify the parts of speech (e.g. d, Aj, N, V, etc.), and write the appropriate abbreviation underneath each item.

2. Identify the words that go together as modifiers and headwords. Put *round* brackets around these sequences or phrases. Each phrase should contain one headword. There need not be any modifier, but there may be three or four. Remember that prepositions, conjunctions and interjections are marked with an *x*. Conjunctions and interjections usually fall outside the bracketed phrases.

3. Label the phrases that you have bracketed (e.g. NP, VP, AjP, AvP, PP). Most phrases are named after their headword (the exception is the PP which consists of a preposition and a NP). These abbreviations go below and in front of the opening bracket.

As an example, these steps are followed for part of a sentence below, taken from Sheila Mackay's novel *Mountain Music,* an extract from which is in the SCOTS corpus (Document 1440):

I could see the driver clearly through the windscreen mirror.

Step 1 (Identifying parts of speech)

I   could see the driver clearly through the windscreen mirror.
pn a   V   d   N   Av   pr   d   N   N

Step 2 (Identifying modifiers and headwords)

H   M   H   M H   H   x   M   M   H
(I)   (could see) (the driver) (clearly) (through the windscreen mirror.)
pn   a   V   d   N   Av   pr   d   N   N

Step 3 (Labelling phrases)

H   M   H   M   H   H   x   M   M   H
(I) (could see) (the driver) (clearly) (through the windscreen mirror.)
NP pn VP a   V NP d   N   AvP Av PP pr   d   N   N

Now try these sentences, also taken from Sheila Mackay's Mountain Music:

(a)   My entire being concentrated on the task.

(b)   In my agitation, I lost control.

(c)   The car somersaulted.

(d)   The roof hit the rock.

(e)   Everything went black.

(f)   A nurse leaned impatiently over me.

(g)   I stared at her in astonishment.

(h)   Dried blood coloured my hair red.

(i)   A large yellow-blue-black bruise had spread over my right cheek and round my eye.

(j)   That skeletal image might have been my reality.

Activity 2

Consider the sentences below. Imagine how you would explain to someone, using accurate grammatical terminology, why one sentence sounds perfectly acceptable, and the other does not:

  1. She ordered a very large whisky.
  2. She ordered a very malt whisky.

How would you explain to a learner of English as a second language how the following phrases are constructed and what they mean?

Yes, I would say it's *very Perth* as well, to be skint.

He doesn't seem *very rock and roll*, does he, Jasper Carrott.

Chapter 6   Describing Complex Phrases

6.0 About this Chapter
6.1 Co-ordination of Words and Phrases
6.2 Subordination of Phrases
6.3 Types of Embedded Phrase
6.3.1 Prepositional Phrases within Noun Phrases
6.3.2 Noun Phrases and Adjective Phrases as Modifiers
6.3.3 Nouns in Apposition
6.3.4 Distinguishing Embedded Elements from Discontinuous Elements
6.4 Summary
6.5 Activities

6.0   About this Chapter

One characteristic feature of the grammar of most languages is that different structures are not simply strung together in a linear fashion. We also embed structures inside other structures. In this chapter, we take our first sustained look at how embedding occurs. We first contrast the stringing together of different structures (co-ordination) with the embedding of one structure inside another (subordination). We then look at some characteristic types of embedded phrase, before considering the practical issue of how to distinguish between embedded elements and discontinuous grammatical structures.

6.1   Co-ordination of Words and Phrases

So far, with a few exceptions, we have dealt with *simple* phrases, that is phrases that contain one headword, and a variable number of modifiers. However, most English phrases are *complex* – that is, phrases that are either (i) linked together using a coordinating conjunction, or (ii) embedded one inside another.

The easier of the two ways to make phrases more complicated is simply to add them together, using a co-ordinating conjunction such as *and, but* or *or*. And so, we can say things like *the bill and the draft regulations would give them a framework.* In saying this, we join together the two NPs *the bill* and *the draft regulations.* We can show words or phrases linked together by co-ordinating conjunctions by using angle brackets <…>:

```
          M  H     x      M  M      H
1.        <(The bill)  and    (the draft regulations)>
          NP d  N     c   NP d  N      N
```

The angle brackets here show that we have a sequence made up of two NPs, linked by the co-ordinating conjunction *and*.

Sometimes it is important to think about where angle brackets are placed when joining sequences of words together. Consider the following sentence:

2.   **The working group is [...] to address *the draft regulations and guidance.***

This sentence could in fact be ambiguous: it could mean that only the regulations were in draft, or it could mean that both the regulations and the guidance were in draft form. We can use the angle brackets to show how much of the phrase the noun modifier *draft* applies to in each possible interpretation of the phrase:

```
          M     M     H       x     H
2a.     (the <draft regulations and guidance>)
        NP d     N     N       c     N


          M  M         H       x     H
2b.     (the draft <regulations and guidance>)
        NP d  N         N       c     N
```

Notice that in the above examples the angled brackets do not necessarily correspond to the boundaries of an individual phrase. In (2a) they show that the two elements linked as a whole are *draft regulations* and *guidance*. In this analysis, the guidance is not necessarily in draft. In (2b), the elements linked are *regulations* and *guidance,* and the analysis suggests that the words *the* and *draft* modify both of the linked headwords, i.e. we assume that the guidance is also in draft.

One observation to be made about this example is that in formal, legal language great care must be taken to avoid ambiguity, and so, at times, legislators can appear to be needlessly explicit. The SCOTS corpus contains a great deal of written parliamentary discourse of a legal nature. The need for unambiguous communication is evident in examples such as the following, in which *draft* is repeated to avoid misunderstanding:

3.   **...the system as laid out in *the draft bill and draft legislation* would allow them to continue to use their own committees and procedures for civic government licensing.**

Different types of phrase can be co-ordinated by *and, but* and *or,* e.g.

4.   ...people's appearances can change,

x   x   H   x   x   H
<either (by accident) or (by design)>.
    c   pr   N   c   pr   N

Here two prepositional phrases, *by accident* and *by design*, together form a single but complex sequence, linked by the conjunction *either...or*. Again, we can use angle brackets to show the coordination of words and phrases.

6.2   Subordination of Phrases

A powerful concept in the analysis of grammar is that of *subordination,* or the embedding of one grammatical constituent, like a phrase, inside another. This is so frequent that we have actually already encountered it in the previous chapter, when looking at Adjective Phrases and Genitive Phrases. Here we demonstrate in more detail how it applies generally to phrase structure (that is, how it applies to the combination of modifiers and headword that make up the phrase). Subordination is one of the most important grammatical concepts you will encounter. In order to understand subordination, you need to have a good grasp of the earlier Chapters. You also need to get into the habit of looking closely at the *meanings* of grammatical structures.

The opening paragraphs below, of an interview with Michael Stipe, conducted by Paul English for the *Daily Record* (SCOTS Document 1620), exhibit a perfectly normal level of subordination for English, but even so many of them are grammatically quite complex.

5.   **Michael Stipe is refreshed. It's 1pm and the jet-lagged REM frontman is picking at a brunch of boiled eggs, melon slices and berries.**

    'I'm not big on breakfast,' he says. 'I got up late today. 'But I think I'm awake now.' The lead singer of the US stadium rockers, once dubbed the biggest band in the world, looks typically moody as he sits in a Kensington hotel room.

    His expression is deadpan, framed with a pair of Woody Allen specs, like an outsized comedy accessory engulfing his small features. A salt-and-pepper carpet of stubble covers his boney face and he speaks in a soft, throaty murmur - nothing like the singing voice the world knows so well.

'I had a day off yesterday which I was so happy with,' he says. 'I needed it.'

But the rest isn't the only reason the 44-year-old is refreshed.

After spending a quarter of a century as the figurehead of a global phenomenon, he has finally been able to put the 'strain' of selling 50 million albums behind him.

'I found it really liberating to release the *Best Of* album last year,' says the enigmatic singer, referring to *In Time: The Best of REM 1988-2003*.

'In some ways it summarised the work people know us best for.

'So when I wrote this stuff I didn't feel the new songs were sitting on my shoulder, saying, 'You have to be as good as we are.' I love a song like *Man On The Moon*. I loved writing it and I love performing it. It's an astonishing piece of music. But I don't have to remember that every time I go to write a new song.

'Releasing the *Best Of* was one of the things that spurred me into a period of prolific writing, the likes of which I'd never experienced before.'

The band's PR arrives and hands him a double espresso.

'Jesus,' he says. 'What are you trying to do, kill me?'

What distinguishes these sentences from most of those we have been dealing with up to now? One answer is that their phrase structure allows the *embedding* of phrases and larger constituents inside other phrases. Some of the phrases that include embedded elements (in *italics*) are:

5a	a brunch *of boiled eggs...*
5b	The lead singer *of the US stadium rockers*
5c	the biggest band *in the world*
5d	a pair *of Woody Allen specs*
5e	A salt-and-pepper carpet *of stubble*
5f	the singing voice *the world knows so well*
5g	a day off yesterday *which I was so happy with*
5h	the only reason *the 44-year-old is refreshed*
5i	a quarter *of a century*
5j	the figurehead *of a global phenomenon*

5k	the 'strain' *of selling 50 million albums*
5l	the work *people know us best for*
5m	an astonishing piece *of music*
5n	every time *I go to write a new song*
5o	a period *of prolific writing*

So far, we have thought of phrases largely as a sequence of *words*, some of which are modifiers and some of which are headwords. All words are elements of a lower *rank*, or lower level of grammar, than a phrase. That is to say, we tend to find words inside phrases, not phrases inside words. But a *complete phrase* can also act as a constituent of another phrase – in other words, a full phrase can, like a single word, go inside another phrase and act as a modifier or a headword in that phrase.

The sole instance of this kind of embedded phrase that we have so far encountered is the Genitive Phrase (5.4.4), which, as we saw in the last chapter, functions as a modifier in another phrase. An example of a Genitive phrase is

```
      M  M   H     H
5p.   (  (the band's) PR)
      NP GP d   N     N
```

Here, the Genitive Phrase *the band's* modifies the headword of the Noun Phrase, *PR*. The Genitive Phrase could be substituted by a single determiner, like *their*. Since embedded phrases function like single words, we sometimes say they are *rank-shifted*; in other words, by acting as a modifier or headword within another phrase, they shift in rank from phrase level to word level in the grammatical hierarchy.

6.3   Types of Embedded Phrase

Let us turn now to different examples of embedded phrases acting as modifiers inside other phrases. The examples are not exhaustive, but they do illustrate the principles by which one phrase is subordinated to another.

6.3.1   Prepositional Phrases within Noun Phrases

If you look at the examples taken from the interview with Michael Stipe, above, it will be clear that many examples of rank-shifting, subordination, or embedding (all three terms describe exactly the same basic process) occur when a Prepositional Phrase is embedded within a Noun Phrase. The embedded PP functions as a modifier in the host NP:

```
           M
       (...  (...) )
       NP   PP
```

e.g.

```
       M   M   H   M x M   M    M      H
5b.    (The lead singer   (of the US stadium rockers))
       NP d  N   N   PP pr d  N    N      N
```

Effectively, the possibility of embedding means that if you find a PP in a sentence you are analysing, you must ask yourself if it is a phrase in its own right or if it is *subordinate to a word* (e.g. acting as a modifier to a noun). Consider the role of the PPs in the sentences below, both taken from SCOTS data:

6. I think we'll have coffee *in the garden*
7. The sunshine *in the garden* had weakened

In (6), the PP answers the question '*Where* will we have coffee?' The PP is not acting as a modifier to any of the other words in the sentence.

In (7) the PP is more closely associated with the head of the NP – indeed the PP identifies *which* area of sunshine was weakening – namely, 'the sunshine in the garden'. The PP thus functions like a determiner in that it identifies the sunshine.

In example (7), then, like *the lead singer of the US stadium rockers,* the PP must be placed *within* the NP brackets as an embedded constituent. The whole embedded PP functions as an M, and therefore it is labelled so, above the line. But it also has its own phrase structure, and that is indicated by the x, M and H within the PP. The NP in example (7) therefore has an overall structure of (MHM). The first modifier is the determiner, *the,* and the second modifier is the PP *in the garden*, which in turn has the structure (xMH):

```
       M    H      M x M  H
7.     (The sunshine   (in the garden)) had weakened
       NP d   N      PP pr d  N
```

Note the position of the brackets in the NP: the brackets of the main phrase do not close until *after* the brackets of the embedded phrase.

There is, of course, the possibility of multiple subordination. The example below from the SCOTS corpus shows an example of a sequence of embeddings:

```
       M   M   H   M  x   M  H      M  x  M H   M x H
8.    (the main room   (in the house   (with a TV     (in it))))
  NP  d   Aj   N  PP pr  d   N     PP  pr   d N  PP pr pn
```

The modification of a noun can take place either before it (pre-modification) or after it (post-modification). The choice of whether to use a pre-modifier or a post-modifier is a stylistic decision, as the following examples from the SCOTS corpus show:

9. **I am sure that deaf and *hearing impaired people* will also appreciate it.**

10. **to raise awareness of the problems that *people with hearing impairments* face**

In example (9) the noun *people* is pre-modified by *hearing impaired,* while in example (10) the same noun is post-modified by an embedded Prepositional Phrase, *with hearing impairments.*

6.3.2   NP's and AjP's as Modifiers

Direct subordination also occurs with AjPs and NPs, both of which can have a modifying function. The commonest functions of an Aj are (i) as a pre-modifier (***mouldy** bread*), or (ii) as a headword that occurs after certain types of verb (e.g. *The bread looks **mouldy***). Adjectives are sometimes piled up in sequence, as below:

```
          M      M       M            M          H
11.    (bonnie, wee, bright-coloured, sparkling things)
  NP   Aj     Aj      Aj          Aj         N
```

In this case it is clear that all the adjectives modify the noun, *things.* We could subtract one or two of them and still have a phrase with an acceptable structure. However, sometimes the function of an adjective is less clear-cut:

```
12.    a  significant skills shortage
       d     Aj        N      N
```

This could be paraphrased as either

```
        M   H    M  x    M          H
12a.   ( a shortage  (of significant skills))
  NP   d    N    PP pr    Aj         N
```

91

or

```
         M    M        H    M x  H
12b.    ( a  significant  shortage  ( of  skills))
        NP d    Aj         N    PP pr  N
```

It can be seen from the bracketing of (12a) and (12b) that the phrase is ambiguous because it is not clear which noun *significant* modifies. The ambiguity can be shown by bracketing the phrase in two ways.

```
        M M  M         H      H
12c.    ( a   (significant  skills)  shortage)
        NP d NP   Aj          N      N
```

```
        M  M          H  M  H
12d.    ( a  significant   (skills shortage))
        NP d    Aj         NP N  N
```

In (12c) the headword *shortage* is pre-modified by a determiner, *a,* and an embedded NP, *significant skills.* The embedded NP also has its own structure, a modifier, the Aj *significant,* and a headword, the N *skills.* In (12d) the bracketing reveals a different meaning. Here the modifiers *a* and *significant* pre-modify a headword which is itself a NP, *skills shortage.* The embedded NP again has its own structure, a modifying N *food,* and a headword, the N *shortage.*

Notice that the two ways of bracketing the NP disambiguate the two possible meanings. The key difference lies in which element of the NP the Aj *significant* is modifying – the *skills* or the *shortage*?

Embedding also commonly occurs when an Aj is modified by a degree Av, as in:

```
        M  M  M  H    H
13.     ( a    (very amusing)  speech)
        NP d  AjP  Av  Aj    N
```

In this case subordination has to be marked because *very* modifies the Aj but does not directly modify the N.   This is evident if we subtract the Aj, because we are then left with

14.   * a very speech.

Ambiguity can also occur within AjPs:

15. **We need more regional representation**

The double meaning of this can be shown by the following paraphrases:

15a. We need representation that is more regional in quality.
15b. We have regional representation but we need a greater quantity of it.

The different meanings of the paraphrases can also be shown by analysing the original sentence in two ways. The analyses below match the meanings given directly above:

		M	**M**	**H**	**H**
15a.	**(We) (need)**	**(**	**(more**	**regional)**	**representation)**
	NP AjP Av			**Aj**	**N**

15a. **(We) (need)   ((more regional) representation)**
     NP AjP Av   Aj   N

15b.
```
             M      M      H
15b.  (We) (need)  (more regional representation)
       NP    d      Aj        N
```

Here the ambiguity resides in the fact that *more* can function in one of two ways in this phrase – either as a degree adverb modifying an adjective, *more regional* (15a), or as a determiner modifying a noun, *more representation* (15b). Each analysis is grammatically correct. The ambiguity is probably resolved in actual communication by the linguistic context – or by the fact that here the meanings are sufficiently close that the listener (in this case to a Scottish Parliamentary debate) engages in 'shallow processing', that is, choosing which of the two senses makes most sense at the time. In the above case, the fuller linguistic context is as follows:

15c. **We need a longer-term approach to secure a change in the way in which the European Union conducts its business in fishing and in other areas. *We need more regional representation* and more rights for regions and for nations to ensure that decisions that are made at a European level are properly implemented locally. Those are our objectives in the shorter and longer terms. I believe that they are right.**

Which of the two analyses do you think is more plausible in this context, and why?

6.3.3 Nouns in Apposition

A further case where embedding occurs is in *apposition*, where one NP is *defined* by another, as in:

M H **M** H
16. **Much was said today about (the First Minister, (Donald Dewar.))**
NP d N **NP** N

For convenience, the first NP is always taken as the main phrase, and the second NP is treated as a post-modifier. For convenience, too, proper names (*Donald Dewar*) and titles (*First Minister*) are treated as single nouns, though the latter could be treated as determiner plus a noun.

6.3.4 Distinguishing Embedded Elements from Discontinuous Elements

As we have seen, adverbs can modify adjectives and so form Adjective Phrases that are then embedded in Noun Phrases, such as the example given as (13) above, and reprinted below:

M **M M H** H
13. **(a (very amusing) speech)**
NP d **AjP Av Aj** N

Adverbs and Adverb Phrases also pop up inside Verb Phrases – but not as modifiers. Because adverbs and Adverb Phrases are quite mobile, they frequently appear in between auxiliary verbs and main verbs, as we can see, for example, if we do a concordance search in the SCOTS corpus for *can *ly*. Some of the results are shown below:

17. **Very few people can *actually* understand pure Urdu...**
18. **We can *certainly* add universities that are not on the academia list...**
19. **This activity can *easily* be varied...**
20. **I can *hardly* believe Christmas is here...**

Although these adverbs look as if they are modifying the main verb, they are actually modifying the *entire* Verb Phrase, or sometimes the clause as a whole. As a result, they can usually be moved from their present position to a position elsewhere in the clause, e.g.

17a. *Actually,* very few people can understand pure Urdu...
18a. We *certainly* can add universities that are not on the academia list...
19a. This activity can be varied *easily*...
20a. I *hardly* can believe Christmas is here...

In these cases, then, we do not have an adverb or an Adverb Phrase *embedded* in a VP; rather we have an adverb or an Adverb Phrase *interrupting* a VP. We can show the analysis of an interrupted VP like this:

	S M	M	H	H	P M	A	H	H		O	M	H

17. **MCl [((Very few) people) (can (actually) understand) (pure Urdu)]**
    NP **AjP** Av Aj N   **VP a** AvP Av   **V**   NP Aj N

Here the lines link the auxiliary verb and the headword in the VP that is being interrupted by the AvP. The AvP is *not* labelled as a modifier in the VP. Compare the embedded AjP *(very few)* inside the NP, which *is* labelled as a modifier in the NP.

The distinction between embedded phrases and phrases that interrupt other phrases casts light on a basic principle of subordination at phrase level – the subordinate constituent has to function as a modifier, or sometimes headword, in the main phrase. Otherwise, like *actually* in the VP above, it continues to function as a full phrase in its own right.

6.4   Summary

This Chapter and the next deal mainly with *subordination*, or the way in which one grammatical constituent can be embedded inside another, effectively shifting its grammatical rank. A full phrase, therefore, can function in the same way as a single word, namely, as a modifier or headword in a larger phrase. We can show embedding by different means. The means preferred in this book is bracketing, although other grammar books use tree diagrams. Both bracketing and tree diagrams show essentially similar information in different ways.

6.5   Activities

Subordination, embedding or rank-shifting, can be initially quite a tricky concept, but with some practice and thought it can quickly be grasped. The basic idea is that grammatical constituents are not simply ordered in sequences, phrase after phrase or clause after clause. A phrase or clause can be embedded *inside* another phrase or clause. The consequence of this grammatical possibility is that some elements of a phrase will themselves have their own phrase structure. And so a modifier within a NP, for example, might itself have the structure of an AjP, a NP or a PP. The activities below will help you to identify examples of subordination at phrase level.

Activity 1   Phrases inside Phrases

Look at the analysis of the NP below:

```
M  H  M x M   M   H
(the girl    (in the yellow bikini))
NP d  N  PP pr d     Aj   N
```

Note that the embedded PP functions as a modifier of the headword, *girl*. Therefore the entire PP is part of the same NP as *the girl*. But the PP also has its own structure, and its own headword, *bikini*. The structure of *both* the main phrase and the subordinate phrase are shown.

From phrases 1-7 below, identify:

a)   one ambiguous Noun Phrase
b)   two Noun Phrases containing an embedded Adjective Phrase
c)   two Noun Phrases containing an embedded Prepositional Phrase
d)   one Adjective Phrase containing an embedded Prepositional Phrase
e)   one Noun Phrase with an embedded Genitive Phrase

1.   an extremely enjoyable reading
2.   a house with a stone stair
3.   a doctor's line
4.   a dog wi twa tails
5.   quite lucky with our neighbours
6.   a very good job
7.   more affordable rented homes

Activity 2
Once you have identified the phrase structures in Activity 1, analyse the whole phrase.

Activity 3
Analyse the following phrases, extracted from the interview with Michael Stipe, earlier in this section:

1. The lead singer of the US stadium rockers
2. the biggest band in the world
3. a pair of Woody Allen specs
4. A salt-and-pepper carpet of stubble
5. a quarter of a century
6. the figurehead of a global phenomenon
7. an astonishing piece of music
8. a period of prolific writing

96

Chapter 7   Combining Phrases Into Clauses

7.0   About this Chapter

In this book, we have slowly been working up the grammatical hierarchy that leads from the morpheme, the smallest grammatical constituent, to the sentence, which is the largest. We have looked at how morphemes combine to form words, and how words combine to form phrases. Now we turn to the combination of phrases into clauses. The analysis of clauses involves identifying how phrases function together, for example as Subjects and Objects. We consider the elements of the clause and some of the issues that arise in the analysis of clauses. To begin, we revisit two of the key concepts in linguistic description, namely the consideration of the formal and functional properties of grammatical constituents.

7.1   Form and Function Revisited

So far, we have mainly thought about form and function in terms of how they can be used to classify words and phrases. As far as form is concerned, for example, we saw earlier that some words have characteristic affixes, e.g. words ending in -*ly* tend to be adverbs. This is a formal test of the word class, and although it is useful it is not necessarily foolproof: *nervously, hopefully, happily,* and *soulfully* are all adverbs, but *portly* is an adjective. A quick concordance search for *weekly* in the SCOTS corpus shows us that it is used much more frequently as an adjective (in phrases like ***weekly income***) than as an adverb (in constructions like ***make decisions daily, weekly, monthly and annually***).

An example of a functional test of a word's class is to ask what other words it can combine with. Only nouns (or other words functioning as nouns) can be modified by *a, an,* or *the.* Only verbs can be modified by auxiliaries like *can, must, should,* and so on.

Accordingly, we have in earlier sections attached different kinds of labels to words in sentences. These are

Form labels: N, V, Aj, Av, d, a, pn, pr, c, i, n

Function labels: M, H

The form label denotes the part of speech of a word and is placed below it. The function label denotes its *role* in the sentence and is placed above it.

```
       M  M  M    H                        Function labels
1.     (a  big black moustache)
       NP d  Aj  Aj    N                   Form labels
```

The *functional* description of an individual word can guide us in the *formal* classification of a phrase; for example, a noun phrase can be formally described as a phrase that has a noun functioning as its headword. Since determiners modify nouns in noun phrases, it follows that we can categorise as a noun *any* term that follows a determiner and functions as its headword, even if that word more commonly appears as another part of speech, like the auxiliary verb *must* in:

```
                          M H
2.     a Scottish Youth Parliament is   (a must)
                          NP d  N
```

In example (2), we can argue, the verb has been turned into a noun meaning something like 'a necessary thing'. We can use the headwords to assign form labels to most phrases: NP, VP, AjP, AvP, etc. The exception, of course, is the PP, which begins with a preposition, but the preposition, you will remember, functions as neither modifier nor headword in the phrase. Rather, the preposition functions to turn a NP into a PP and signals the relationship of the PP to the rest of the sentence. Like the form labels of individual words, we place the form labels of phrases *below* the sentence.

Like individual words, phrases have functions as well as forms. That is to say, phrases relate to other phrases in different ways. For example, the phrase *many people* functions in two different ways in the following two sentences, from different Scottish Parliamentary debates in the SCOTS corpus (sentence 3 is slightly adapted):

3.   this reduction in service affects many people

4.   **many people purchase cigarettes over the internet**

In Sentence (4) the plural NP *many people* has a relationship of concord, or agreement, with the plural VP, *purchase*, while in Sentence (3) it doesn't (when there is a relationship of concord between two phrases, they must agree in number – that is, when one phrase is singular or plural, the other must 'agree' and be singular or plural too). In sentence (1) the concord is between the singular NP *this reduction in service* and the singular VP *affects*.

The lack/presence of concord between the VPs and the NP *many people* in Sentences (3) and (4) suggests that the NP *many people* has a different function in each sentence. This Chapter will deal mainly with the different functions that phrases perform when they combine to form what we call *clauses* in English.

7.2   SPOCA

Phrases have five possible functions in the clause: *Subject (S), Predicator (P), Object (O), Complement (C), Adverbial (A)*. A useful mnemonic for these is **SPOCA**, which indicates the order in which these phrase functions normally occur in the clause. The five functions are defined and exemplified briefly below, and then considered in detail throughout the rest of this Chapter.

7.2.1   Subject

The **Subject** of a clause is defined as that phrase which has a relationship of concord, or agreement, with the VP. Consider the clauses below:

5. **This situation *creates* tension for many teachers.**

6. **Writers *create* meaning by the way in which they present their text visually.**

Each clause begins with a NP, a singular one and a plural one respectively. The Verb Phrase (*creates/create*) changes in order to agree with that NP in the clause, and it agrees only with that NP. This relationship of agreement, or concord, identifies the Subject.

Formally, Subjects are often NPs, they tend to precede the VP in a clause, and they usually (but don't always) express the person or thing responsible for the action of the verb – but it is the *functional* relationship of concord that is the key to defining the Subject.

Dummy Subjects in existential clauses
As noted above, Subjects usually precede VPs in the clause in English. However, sometimes we want to shift the information that is in the Subject to the end of a clause. In such cases, we use a *dummy Subject* to mark the usual place of the Subject, before the NP, and the actual Subject, which is either a phrase or a full clause (see the discussion of Noun Clauses later, in Chapter 8.5.2), is moved to the end of the clause. This shift happens when we simply wish to indicate the existence of things, in clauses beginning *there is/are.* For example, instead of saying –

```
              S            P    A
7.     MCl [ (Some bushes) (are) (in the garden)]
          NP              VP    PP
```

– we can replace the Subject with the dummy Subject *there,* and say:

```
          S x    P H S M     H    A x  M  H
7a.    MCl [ (There)  (are) (some bushes)   (in the garden) ]
          VP V NP d       N    PP pr  d   N
```

In clauses such as (7a), *there* is simply a grammatical marker, which is why it is not given any form label, and its function is marked with an 'x'. The function of the grammatical marker here is to occupy the normal Subject position, while the real Subject, *some bushes,* has been moved to a position after the Verb Phrase. The analysis shows both Subjects, the dummy *there* and the full *some bushes.*

7.2.2 Predicator

The **Predicator** in a clause is *always* the Verb Phrase. The VP is the constituent around which the clause 'revolves'. Each full clause *must* have a Verb Phrase functioning as Predicator, and a Predicator by itself can constitute a full clause, as we can see in this exchange between a mother

(F1113) and her young daughter (F1114) from the SCOTS corpus. The daughter's final command – *Catch!* – functions as a full clause by itself.

8.   **F1113: What are you goin to do then?**
        F1114: Catch.
        F1113: Catch.
        F1114: [laugh] //[inhale]//
        F1113: //Okay.//
        F1114: Catch! [laugh]

We could analyse the clause as follows: **MCl [(Catch!)]**

with **P H** above and **VP V** below.

7.2.3 Object

The **Object** of a clause is that constituent (usually a NP) which has the potential to be the Subject...but isn't. In other words, there is *no* relationship of concord, or agreement, between an Object and the VP, but if you rewrote the clause, there could be. For example, there is no relation of agreement between the plural VP *create* and the singular VP *meaning* in the clause we looked at above:

6. **Writers *create* meaning by the way in which they present their text visually.**

We can, however, rephrase this clause as follows:

6a. Meaning *is created* by the way in which writers present their text visually.

In (6a) *Meaning* has become the Subject of the clause (it now agrees with the singular verb, *is created*). Therefore, in (6) *meaning* is the Object of the clause: it has no agreement with the verb phrase, but it has the *potential* to become the Subject if the clause is rephrased as it is in (6a).

7.2.4 Complement

Not all verbs can be followed by Objects. In some sentences the VP is followed by a NP or AjP which is not the Subject, and such phrases do *not* have the potential ever to become Subject. These constituents are called **Complements**. They usually describe or identify other NPs in the sentence. You can find examples in the SCOTS corpus by looking up verbs that are usually followed by complements, namely verbs of *being* like *be* and *become*, and certain verbs of sensory perception like *seems, looks, tastes, feels, sounds, smells, e.g.*

9. **I'll become your sports reporter.**

10. **Oh, that smells lovely!**

Here the NP *your sports reporter* and the AjP *lovely* do not have the potential to become Subject of the clause. You cannot rephrase these clauses as:

9a. *Your sports reporter will be become by me.
10a. *Lovely is smelled by that!

Therefore, the NP and AjP are not Objects but Complements. Since they describe the Subject of the sentence, they are sometimes referred to as Subject Complements.

Complements can also appear in sentences that contain an Object, and they may describe the Object rather than the Subject. In such cases they may be referred to as Object Complements. However, Object Complements still cannot become the Subject of a sentence. Only a small number of verbs can be followed by both Objects and Object Complements. A SCOTS corpus search for *call*, paint** results in a few examples:

11. **I called him *grandad.***
12. **I painted them *white* for Halloween.**

In (11) the NP *grandad* is functioning as the Object Complement in the sentence – it describes, or in this case names, the Object, *him*. In (12), the AjP *white* is an Object Complement describing *them* (which in the context of the conversation, turn out to be wellington boots).

The different grammatical roles of Object and Complement are particularly clear in these examples. In each case, the Object of the clause can become the Subject, but the Complement cannot, e.g.

11a. He was called grandad by me.
11b. *Grandad was called him by me.
12a. They were painted white by me for Halloween.
12b. *White was painted them by me for Halloween.

7.2.5 Adverbial

The final function which a phrase can perform is that of **Adverbial.** Remember to distinguish Adverb (a type of word) and Adverb Phrase (one type of phrase) from Adverb*ial* (a clause function which is performed by different kinds of phrase). Adverbials can be Adverb Phrases, Prepositional Phrases or even, in some cases, Noun Phrases. They give extra information about the action or event in the clause – e.g. where, when, why, how it happened. But the two main ways to recognise an Adverbial are (i) that it is extremely *mobile*: you can often move this constituent into different positions in the sentence; and (ii) it is often *inessential*: you can usually omit the Adverbial and the sentence will still make sense. A fully-analysed clause, containing several Adverbials, is shown below:

	A x	M	H	**S**	M	H	**P** M	M	H
13.	**Cl [(By this time)**			**(some passengers)**			**(had been helped)**		
	PP pr	d	N	**NP** d		N	**VP** a	a	V

	A x	M	M	H	x	x	H
	<(to the boat deck) and (into lifeboats.)>]						
	PP pr	d	N	N	c	**PP** pr	N

This sentence illustrates the fact that a clause may contain several Adverbials: here three Prepositional Phrases, the last two of which are joined together into a single unit by the conjunction *and*. All of the Adverbials are inessential – you could omit them all and still have a brief but acceptable sentence, *Some passengers had been helped.* Many Adverbials are mobile constituents, although moving Adverbials may well produce subtle variations in meaning, as below, where there is perhaps less immediate emphasis on the time in which this event happened:

13a. Some passengers, *by this time*, had been helped to the boat deck and into lifeboats.
13b. Some passengers had been helped to the boat deck and into lifeboats, *by this time.*

7.3   Typical Clause Structures

Once we start combining phrases according to the rules given above, we have a *clause*. A clause is essentially a grammatical *combination of phrases*, so when we are talking about SPOCA analyses, we are really talking about clause structure.

Below are some examples of typical clause analyses, showing clauses with a variety of SPOCA variations. Note that the basic **SPOC** sequence is quite rigid in contemporary English; Adverbials, however, can pop up in several places in a clause:

Clause type	A	S	A	P	O	C	A
P				Catch!			
PO				Catch	it!		
POA				Catch	the ball		now!
SP		She		snores.			
SPO		He		loves	his dog.		
SPC		Defeat		tastes		bitter.	
ASAPOA	Happily	they	quickly	found	him		again.
ASAPCA	However	rivals	often	become		friends	in time.

7.4   Clauses and sentences

In this book, we use square brackets [....] to identify clauses. As the above table shows clearly, the key characteristic of a full clause is that it *must* contain a VP functioning as Predicator. When we combine clauses, either by adding them together using conjunctions or punctuation, or by embedding clauses inside one another, we produce sentences, the highest-ranking grammatical constituent. Since each full sentence must contain at least one clause, and each clause must contain a Predicator, then it follows that sentences must contain one or more Predicators. Sentences that contain only one Predicator – like all the examples given in the table above – are one-clause or *simple* sentences. It follows from this that a grammatically complete sentence must also contain at least one Predicator.

Most sentences, of course, contain more than one clause, like the one below, which is a *compound* sentence containing two clauses. Compound sentences are linked by coordinating conjunctions, like *and, or, nor, but*:

```
           A  H   S  H    P    H     O M    H        x
14.    MCl [ (Later,) (cycling) (broadened)  (my horizons)]  and
          AvP Av  NP N   VP   V      NP d     N             c


           P  H     O H  A x   M       M     H      H
       MCl [ (took)  (me)  (to   (further off) places.)]
          VP  V   NP pn PP pr AjP  Av     Aj    N
```

104

It is worth looking at this compound sentence in a some detail. The two Predicators have been highlighted in **bold.** The Subject of the first clause *cycling* is carried over to the second clause, which has no explicit Subject of its own. The first clause begins with an Adverbial (realised by an Adverb Phrase), and the second clause ends with one (realised by a Prepositional Phrase). Each clause has an Object, realised by a Noun Phrase. In the second clause the headword of the Noun Phrase is realised by a pronoun. In the same clause, the concluding Prepositional Phrase includes an embedded Adjective Phrase, which modifies the final noun.

This sentence, then, which is not particularly complex, gives a sense of how grammatical complexity works in English grammar. Words combine into phrases, phrases into clauses, and clauses into sentences. At the same time, clauses and phrases can be linked and embedded, one inside the other, to pack a considerable amount of information into the unified grammatical structure that we call the sentence.

Before turning to a detailed consideration of subordination at clause level, that is what happens when one clause is embedded inside another, let us conclude this section by reviewing and refining some of our observations about the clause itself.

7.5   Clause Function and Word Order

In English, grammatical function is closely related to word order. As noted above in relation to the table of typical clause structures, the normal order of constituents in an English clause is **SPOC,** with the **A** occupying various possible slots in the clause. Every full clause contains a **P** and most clauses contain a **S.** (An exception, as we saw above, is compound sentences where there is often omission of the Subject to avoid repetition.)

	A	S	P	O		x		P	O	A

14a. [Later, cycling broadened my horizons] and [~~cycling~~ took me to further off places.]

Normally the **S** precedes the **P** as in the clauses above. The **O** generally comes after the **P,** as does the **C,** but neither of these elements is obligatory in the clause. **Adverbials** are likewise optional elements, and the possibility of varying their position makes them fairly easy to identify.

The normal order can sometimes be violated for stylistic effect, as in the sentence below, from a song sung in a Scots play, *Bruised Blue* by Cecilia Grainger. In the character's song, the position of **C** before **S** and **P** both emphasises the adjective *sad,* and makes the lyric sound archaic and perhaps even proverbial in nature:

15. **LORI. (Sings):**

```
     x   x  C  H  P H  S M   H    M x M  M      H
  [ Oh, oh  (sad)  (is)  (the fortune (o aw wimmin kind.))]
     i    i  AjP Aj VP V  NP d   N     PP pr d   N      N
```

The Complement is drawn to our attention by placing it before the Subject, in a marked grammatical position. When attention is drawn to a clause element by putting it to the front in this way, the process is known as *marked fronting.* The 'violation' of normal sentence order, then, can mark a grammatical constituent out as important in some way, and it can control the sequence of information conveyed to the listener or reader.

7.6 Subject and Object

The **S** and **O** slots are generally filled by NPs. Most sentences have Subjects; Objects are more optional. There is, as we shall see below, a strong relationship between the presence or absence of an Object, and the kind of Predicator chosen.

```
           S    H        P  H
16.   MCl [ (Dolly Emslie) (snorted.)]
           NP   N        VP  V
```

```
           S    H        P H   O M  H
17.   MCl [ (Mrs Morrison) (rang) (the bell.)]
           NP   N        VP V  NP d   N
```

7.6.1 Transitive and Intransitive verbs

In the above examples, the verb *to snort* does not normally take O (although there are a few instances when it might). The word is therefore normally classified as an *intransitive* (intr) verb. The verb *to ring,* on the other hand, often has O, though not always. Verbs that we expect to be followed by an Object are called *transitive* (tr) verbs.

The word *transitive* comes from Latin. It contains three morphemes:

TRANS - IT - IVE
Prefix   root   suffix

106

The root is from the Latin word *ire* meaning 'to go'. The prefix *trans-* means 'across, beyond' and occurs in many English words, e.g. *trans*port, *trans*action. The morpheme *<-ive>* is a common adjective suffix. A transitive verb could thus be described as one where the meaning 'goes across' from S to O via P. *Intransitive* contains an extra morpheme, the negative prefix *in-*. An intransitive verb is therefore one where the meaning *doesn't* extend from S to O.

This etymology indicates the *semantic role* of S and O (i.e. what they typically mean). S is typically the *agent* in the clause, i.e. it refers to the person, thing, etc. which performs the action denoted by the P. O is typically the *patient*, i.e. the person, thing, etc. affected by the action.

Many English verbs can occur in both transitive and intransitive patterns:

	S	M	H	P H	
18.	**MCl [(The door)**	**(closed)]**			*intransitive use*
	NP d	N	VP V		

	S H	A H	P H	O M H	
19.	**MCl [(I)**	**(gently)**	**(closed)**	**(the door)]**	*transitive use*
	NP pn	AvP A	VP V	NP d N	

Some verbs are *reflexive* verbs, where S and O refer to the same thing:

	S H	A H	P H	O H	
20.	**MCl [(I)**	**(thoroughly)**	**(enjoyed)**	**(myself)]**	*reflexive verb*
	NP pn	AvP Av	VP V	NP pn	

Myself is a *reflexive pronoun*. Verb categories such as transitive, intransitive and reflexive are often given in entries for verbs in dictionaries, e.g. in the entries for the first sense of *scart* and the second and seventh senses of *miss* in the Dictionary of the Scots Language (www.dsl.ac.uk):

Scart, Skart, Skrat, *v.*
1. *tr.* To scratch, lacerate or mark (a person, his (one's own) face, etc.) with the nails, etc.

Miss, *v.*
2. *intr.* To fail to happen (ne. and em.Sc. (a), s.Sc., Uls. 1963). Obs. in Eng.
7. *refl.* in phr. *to miss anesel*, to miss something good or entertaining by one's absence. Gen.Sc.

7.6.2 Direct and Indirect Objects

As we have just seen, some clauses have no Object. Many have one; a few have two. Whether there is one Object or two in the clause, the rule for identifying the Object holds true – all Objects can become the Subject of the clause. As shown below, the verb *tell* can be followed by a single Direct Object (*he told a funny tale*), or by an Indirect and Direct Object (*Jack told me the whole tale*). The clause *he told a funny tale* can be rephrased with the Direct Object as Subject: *a funny tale was told to me*. The second clause could be rephrased with either the Direct Object or the Indirect Object as Subject: *The whole tale was told to me by Jack,* or *I was told the whole tale by Jack.*

```
          S H  P H    O M  M    H
21.   MCl [ (he)  (told)   (a funny tale)]          Direct Object
          NP pn VP V   NP d   Aj    N
```

```
          S H    P H   Oi H  Od M   M    H
22.   MCl [ (Jack) (told)  (me)   (the whole tale)]     Indirect +
          NP N   VP V  NP pn  NP d    Aj    N        Direct Objects
```

It is a rule of English word order that Oi precedes Od. In order to distinguish Od and Oi, we can also apply a *transformation* test, by which we *transform* the clause into an alternative but equally acceptable structure with the same meaning. Oi can be transformed into a PP introduced by the prepositions *to* or *for*:

22a. Jack told the whole tale (to me)

The transformed Object can now be deleted (*Jack told the whole tale*) or moved (*Jack told to me the whole tale*), and so, like other Prepositional Phrases, it functions as an Adverbial.

7.6.3 Object and Complement

COM - PLE - MENT is another word of Latin etymology.
prefix root   suffix

The root *plere* means 'to fill', the prefix *com-* means 'with' and *-ment* is a noun suffix. A *Complement* is thus a *thing* that *fills* or *completes* something. In its non-grammatical sense, the noun is used to mean something like 'quota', and it is found as such in various expressions in the SCOTS corpus:

23. the parliament's full complement of security staff

24. the current total staffing complement of the SQA

In grammar, as noted above, the Complement (**C**) refers to a descriptive phrase (usually an AjP or NP) that follows an intransitive verb, often *be* or *become*, or verbs expressing sensory perception, and it gives us additional information, usually about **S**. If we analyse examples (9) and (10) above in more detail, we get the following:

```
      S H  P M   H      C M    M      H
9.   MCl [ (I)  ('ll become) (your sports reporter.)]
     NP pn VP a   V     NP d    N      N
```

```
      x S  H  P  H      C H
10.  MCl [Oh (that) (smells) (lovely!)]
      i NP N  VP   V    AjP  Aj
```

The Subjects and Predicators here would be semantically incomplete without their Complements: *that smells...; *I'll become....* The range of verbs that take Complements is quite small. Most of them refer to physical or emotional states, e.g. *feel, look, smell, sound, taste, appear, remain, grow,* as in the next examples:

```
      S  M H  P H   C  H
25.  MCl [ (the air) (grew) (chill)]
     NP   d  N VP V  AjP Aj
```

```
      S  M   H     P M   H     C  M       H
26.  MCl [ (this number) (has remained) (relatively constant)]
     NP   d   N    VP a   V     AjP Av       Aj
```

As we saw earlier, we can use a *transformation test* to distinguish O and C. Clauses with O can be transformed from *active* into *passive* structures, while clauses with C cannot. Compare the earlier examples with some reformulations:

```
      S H  P H   O M  M   H
21.  MCl [ (he) (told)  (a funny tale)]          Active voice
     NP pn VP V   NP d   Aj   N
```

```
      S M  M   H  P M H   A x  H
21a. MCl [(a funny tale) (was told)  (by him)]    Passive voice
     NP d  Aj   N VP a  V  PP pr  pn
```

109

```
       S H  P M   H     C M   M     H
9.   MCl [  (I)   (’ll become) (your sports reporter.)]
     NP pn VP a    V     NP  d   N     N
```

```
       S  M     M     H     P M M   H    A x  H
9a.  *MCl [(your sports reporter) (will be become) (by me)]
       NP  d     N     N    VP a  a   V    PP pr pn
```

Verbs, like *taste,* that can be both transitive and intransitive can take either O or C.

```
       S H   P M   H     O M      H
27.  MCl [  (I)   (’ve tasted) (better medicine)]    *Transitive + Object*
     NP pn VP  a   V     NP  Aj      N
```

```
       S M    H     P H    C H
28.  MCl [ (the product) (tasted) (putrid)]          *Intransitive +*
     NP d    N     VP V   AjP Aj                      *Complement*
```

7.6.4 Subject and Object Complements

As noted earlier, the Complement can describe or have a relationship of identity with *either* the Subject *or* the Object of a clause.

```
       S H  P H  Cs H
     MCl [ (I)  (’m)  (Bob)]                        *Subject Complement (Cs)*
29.    NP pn VP V  NP N
```

```
       S   M    H     P H  O H  Co H
30.  MCl [ (Other people) (call) (him) (Bob)]   *Object Complememt (Co)*
     NP    d    N     VP V  NP pn NP  N
```

In the first example C (*Bob*) is equivalent to S (*I*) and so is labelled **Cs**. In the second example, C (*Bob,* again) is now equivalent to O (*him*) and so is labelled **Co**. Where there is an Object Complement, it always follows the Object in the clause.

7.7   Determining the Function of Prepositional Phrases

As we observed earlier, different types of phrase – PPs, AvPs and NPs – can function as Adverbials in a clause. As we have also seen, PPs can function as embedded modifiers in other phrases, such as NPs. If you are unsure whether a PP is Adverbial at clause level, or a modifier within another phrase, it is a good idea to test its *mobility*. Adverbials, as we know, can move around a clause while modifiers must stay within their phrases, as in the following example, which contains two Prepositional Phrases:

```
      A  M  x  M    M      H    S H P  M   H
31.   [ (high on  a terraced hill)    (I)  (could see)
      PP Av pr  d    Aj     N   NP pn VP a    V

      O M H   M  x  M    M      H
      (a house  (with an arched lintel))]
      NP d  N   PP pr  d    Aj     N
```

Compare:

31a. *I could see,* **high on a terraced hill,** *a house with an arched lintel*
31b. *I could see a house with an arched lintel,* **high on a terraced hill**

31c. ***high on a terraced hill,** *I could see,* **with an arched lintel,** *a house*
31d. ***with an arched lintel,** *high on a terraced hill, I could see a house*

Here, the PP *high on a terraced hill* is an Adverbial (in this case a Prepositional Phrase premodified by the intensifying adverb *high*), and so it can be moved quite easily from the beginning to the middle and the end of the sentence. However, the PP *with an arched lintel* is less mobile – in natural English it really must follow 'house', the headword of the phrase in which it acts as a modifier.

7.8   Activities

We saw earlier that words that relate to each other can be combined into phrases. The next step in our grammatical analysis has been to combine related phrases into clauses by showing how they function. We label the *function* of each phrase as Subject, Predicator, Object, Complement or Adverbial (SPOCA).

Three steps suggested for phrase analysis, given at the end of Chapter 5, are copied below:

Step 1 (Identifying parts of speech)

I   could see the driver clearly through the windscreen mirror.
pn   a   V   d   N   Av   pr   d   N   N

Step 2 (Identifying modifiers and headwords)

```
H     M   H   M   H       H     x    M     M        H
(I)   (could see) (the driver) (clearly) (through the windscreen mirror.)
pn    a   V   d   N       Av    pr   d     N         N
```

Step 3 (Labelling phrases)

```
   H     M   H    M   H        H
   (I)  (could see) (the driver)  (clearly)
NP pn  VP a   V  NP d  N     AvP  Av
```

```
      x   M      M        H
   (through the windscreen  mirror.)
PP   pr   d      N         N
```

To these, we can now add a further step, showing the *clause function* of the different phrases. Above and in front of each round-bracketed phrase, label its *function* as S,P,O,C or A. It is often easiest to begin with the Predicator, then identify any related Subject, Object, Complement or Adverbial(s). Put square brackets around each sequence of phrases related to a single Predicator – that is your clause:

```
    S H   P M   H   O M   H
MCl [ (I)  (could see)  (the driver)
    NP pn  VP a   V   NP d   N
```

```
A    H   A   x   M     M        H
   (clearly) (through the windscreen mirror.)]
AvP Av  PP  pr   d     N        N
```

Here we have a clause with the structure SPOAA.

Analysing simple sentences

By this point, you should be able to give full analyses of (a) simple sentences, in other words sentences that consist of a single clause, and (b) compound sentences, consisting of sentences linked by coordinating conjunctions. Try analysing these examples, taken from the children's story *Katie Morag and the Two Grandmothers* by Mairi Hedderwick (SCOTS Document 832):

1. One sunny Wednesday morning Mrs McColl woke Katie Morag early.

2. Here comes the boat.

3. Granma Mainland lived far away in the big city.

4. My, you're still a smart wee Bobby Dazzler.

5. Grannie Island revved the engine very loudly.

6. Show Day was always a big event on the Island of Struay.

7. Alecina was Grannie Island's prize sheep.

8. But all ended well.

Chapter 8   From Clause To Complex Sentence

8.0   About this Chapter

In this chapter we reach the upper limit of grammar, the largest grammatical unit, namely the complex sentence. As complex phrases are formed by embedding one or more phrases inside another, so complex sentences are formed by embedding one or more clauses (subordinate clauses) inside a main clause. This chapter compares sentence types, shows you how to recognise subordinate clauses, and gives examples of different types of subordinate clause. By the time you have finished this chapter, you should be able to parse a wide variety of sentences.

8.1   The Complexity of Sentences

As Chapter 7 showed, when different phrases relate to each other in a meaningful way around a Predicator, then we have a *clause* in English. The heart of any clause is the Predicator, which is always a VP. As we also observed in the previous chapter, most obviously in the table in 7.3, other phrases cluster around the Predicator in different ways. There is usually a phrase functioning as the Subject, which agrees with the Predicator, and perhaps one or more Objects, Complements and/or Adverbials. Whatever the combination of other constituents, it is usually the case that if you have a Predicator, you have a clause.

Single clauses make up what are called *simple* sentences; namely, sentences with one Predicator and usually one or more other phrases too. Our description of grammar could stop there, at the simple sentence. However, most written and spoken English does not consist only of simple sentences, as the two passages below, taken and adapted from an article by Isabel Murray on the fiction of Jessie Kesson, illustrate:

(a) *Adapted version [Predicators italicised]*
[1] We *can enjoy* Jessie Kesson's work. [2] We *can admire* it too. [3] We *do not have to notice* a particular fact about it. [4] Its simplicity *is* very individual, very one-of-a-kind. [5] But her books *are not* traditional stories, with beginnings, middles and ends, in that order. [6] We *can look* just a little deeper. [7] Then we *can see* something. [8] Each *is* individually created within a unique structure. [9] This best *displays* the character(s), and their inmost feelings. [10] Kesson *experimented* with her first and best known novel, 'The White Bird Passes', for over sixteen years or more. [11] During this time, she *discovered* a personal means of expression. [12] Her writing *appears* simple and effortless. [13] A crucially important factor in the construction of each of her novels *is* Kesson's treatment of time, in each case uniquely different, and appropriate to the work.

(b) *Original version [Numbers added and Predicators italicised]*
[14] It *is* possible *to enjoy* and *admire* Jessie Kesson's work without particularly *noticing* that its simplicity *is* very individual, very one-of-a-kind. [15] But her books *are not* traditional stories, with beginnings, middles and ends, in that order: if we *look* just a little deeper we *can see* that each *is* individually created within a unique structure, *to* best *display* the character(s), and their inmost feelings. [16] Over the sixteen or more years when she *was engaged* experimentally in *producing* her first and best known novel, 'The White Bird Passes', Kesson *discovered* her own ways of *expressing* herself, and *made* them *appear* simple and effortless. [17] A crucially important factor in the construction of each of her novels *is* Kesson's treatment of time, in each case uniquely different, and appropriate to the work.

Over the centuries, English prose style has developed into a sophisticated medium for communicating meaning. The two passages above communicate approximately the same meaning, but do so in different ways. Passage (a) consists of thirteen simple sentences – the Predicators are *italicised*, and you can see that each sentence only contains one of them. Passage (b) communicates the same amount of meaning in only four sentences, but these sentences are much more complicated in structure. If you count the *italicised* Predicators in these sentences, you will find that there are two or more in each one. In this Chapter we explore how clauses are linked together and embedded into complex sentences such as these.

Passage (b) makes use of three essential features of English grammar:

Substitution
Instead of referring to nouns repeatedly by name, the writer has used pronouns, eg:

16b. **Kesson discovered *her own ways of expressing herself,* and made**

⟵——————————————|

***them* appear...**

Ellipsis
Ellipsis occurs when an expected grammatical item has been omitted. As we saw in the previous Chapter, in compound sentences when the Subject remains constant, it can be omitted in the second clause:

16b. **Kesson discovered her own ways of expressing herself, and [she] made them appear...**

Compound and complex sentences
Each of the four sentences in version (b) contains more than one Predicator (italicised in the text) and therefore cannot be a simple sentence. Their internal structure includes *linking elements* such as *coordinating conjunctions* (e.g. *and*) and another set of conjunctions called *subordinating conjunctions* (e.g. *if, when, that*). Other complex sentences use *relative pronouns* such as *which, who* and (again, but in a different role) *that.* A great variety of sentence patterns like these is available in English, which makes the language much more flexible. We considered *compound* sentences in the previous Chapter; here, therefore, we shall turn to *complex* sentences.

8.2   Main Clauses and Subordinate Clauses

Basically there are two types of clause, *main (*or *principal) clauses* [MCl] and *subordinate clauses* (or simply *subclauses*) [SCl].

A main clause is an independent unit which can stand alone as a sentence {Se}. Every sentence must have a main clause. Since simple sentences have only one clause, that clause must by definition be a main clause.

```
          S   M   H   P H  x   C   M          H
15b.  Se { MCl [ (Her books) (are not)   (traditional stories.)]}
              NP  d   N  VP V  n  NP   Aj          N
```

117

In contrast, a subordinate clause cannot stand alone as a sentence. Subordinate clauses or 'subclauses' are embedded within other grammatical categories, namely clauses and phrases. A subordinate clause contains further information about some element in the main clause and so is linked to the MCl in some way. One of the subclauses in sentence (16) in the above passage is linked to the main clause by the conjunction *when,* which indicates that the relationship between subclause and main clause is one of time:

16c. ***when* she was engaged experimentally...**

The convention for subclauses is that their brackets are placed *within* those of the main clause so that their status is clearly indicated.

Se{ MCl[......SCl[........]]}

Since subclauses can also be subordinated within other subclauses, bracketing can become quite complicated. A golden rule is that brackets come in pairs; if you open a pair of brackets, you must eventually close it. If you do an analysis and end up with five left-facing brackets and only three right-facing ones, then there is something wrong.

8.3   Conjunctions Revisited

In order to get to grips with subordinate clauses in particular, it is useful first to review some closed-class words, specifically conjunctions, those grammatical words whose job it is mainly to indicate grammatical relationships within the phrase and clause. Closed-class words were introduced in Chapter 3.

Conjunctions link words, phrases and clauses. There are two main types of conjunctions:

(a) co-ordinating conjunctions, e.g. *and, or, nor, but.* These are used to link those grammatical units that are at the same level in the rank scale, i.e. they link words with words, phrases with phrases, and clauses with clauses.

(b) subordinating conjunctions, e.g. *after, although, as, because, before, if, how, however, like, once, since, than, that, though, till, unless, until, when, where, while.*
Some subordinating conjunctions are themselves complex; that is, they consist of more than one word. However, we can treat them as single conjunctions. They include *as far as, as if, in case, in (order) that, rather than, so that,* etc.

Subordinating conjunctions are the set of closed-class words which signal subordinate clauses, and give information about their relationship to the main clause they inhabit. In addition to the two main types of conjunction noted above, *correlative* conjunctions attach to two separate elements. These can also be:

co-ordinating: *both ... and, (n)either ... (n)or*
subordinating: *if ... then, although ... yet*, etc.

Notice, in the many examples below, that when we draw diagrams of sentence structure, the conjunctions sometimes fall outside the round phrase brackets – this is because they *link* phrases; they are not *part of* phrases. Since they are neither headwords nor modifiers in a phrase, we put an x above them to indicate their linking function.

8.4   Comparing Simple, Compound and Complex Sentences

As we have seen, sentences are made up of combinations of clauses (i.e. combinations of phrases functioning as SPOC and/or A). A *simple* sentence contains only one VP functioning as Predicator. *Compound* and *complex* sentences contain more than one Predicator.

In the rest of this Chapter, we shall explore the ways in which clauses can be linked together to make more complicated sentences. These ways include processes of subordination very similar to those we saw in phrases in Chapter 7.

For ease of comparison, the examples below show a simple sentence, a compound sentence and a complex sentence. The clause functions of the *main* clauses (SPOCA) are shown in **bold.**

Simple sentence (one main clause: SPO)

```
          S    H     A M   H     P      H        O M M   H
18. Se{MCl [ (Shetland) (this summer) (demonstrated)   (a clear passion
          NP   N    NP d   N     VP     V        NP d Aj  N

    M x   H
     (for sport.))]}
    PP pr  N
```

119

Compound sentence (four main clauses: SPO, SPA, SPO and SPC)

      S   H   x   H   **P** M H **O** H
19. Se{MCl [<(Houses) and (cars)> (were flying) (flags,)]
         NP N   c NP N VP a   V   NP N

    S H   **P** H   **A**   H
MCl [(tracksuits) (were) (everywhere,)]
  NP   N   VP V AvP Av

    S H **P** M   H   x   H
MCl (bairns) <(were collecting) and (swapping)>
  NP N VP a   V   c VP V

O M H M M   M   H   M x M H
(pin badges (the unofficial currency (of the Games)))]
NP N N PP d   Aj   N   PP pr d   N

  x   **S** M H   x   H M x M M   H   **P** H
and MCl [<(the atmosphere) and (buzz (at the sports venues)>) (was)
  c   NP d   N   c NP N PP pr d   N   N   VP V

C M   H
(truly uplifting.)]
AjP Av   Aj

Complex sentence

The first clause of the compound sentence below (20) contains an Adverbial that is an embedded clause, beginning with the conjunction *if.* The presence of this embedded Adverbial Clause (ACl) makes this also a complex sentence. Its structure is *SPCA+SPC.* The structure of the embedded Adverbial Clause is *SPO.*

      S H **P** M   M H **C** M M   H
20. MCl [(It) (would have been)   (a hollow victory)
       NP pn VP a   a   V NP d   Aj   N

```
A   x  S  H  P  H  O  M  H  M  x  H           x
SCl [if  (we) (had)  (a clutch  (of medals))]]  but
ACl  c NP pn VP V NP  d  N   PP pr  N              c


 S  H   x   H  M  x M    H            P H  C  M   H
MCl [ <(some) or  (all>  (of the organisation)) (was)    (a shambles.)]
     NP  pn   c NP pn PP  pr  d    N              VP V NP d   N
```

The level of detail given in the above example might seem rather offputting at first, but with practice you should be able to read this kind of analysis increasingly easily. If you are having difficulty, train yourself to read this kind of analysis *systematically* – look first at the classification of words (pn, a, V, Aj, etc.), then at the relationship of modifiers to headwords. Pay attention to embedded modifiers like the prepositional phrases *of medals* and *of the organisation*. Remember that angled brackets < > indicate words or phrases linked by a conjunction. And finally, look at the clause structure (SPOCA), noting any embedded clauses functioning as Subject, Object, Complement or Adverbial.

The next few subsections give some advice on recognising subclauses, and introduce you to different types of subclause.

8.5   How to Recognise Subordinate Clauses

Most sentences contain a mixture of MCl and SCl, as in the example of the complex sentence in the subsection above. Subclauses can be found at the beginning, middle or end of a sentence. Remember that the main clause *contains* the subclause as an embedded constituent that performs one of a small number of possible functions.

Subordinate clauses are generally named after the function they perform or the form they have – some function like NPs, some like AvPs and others look rather like PPs. Two types of subordinate clause have more specific functions – comparing and modifying. Accordingly, there are five types of subordinate clauses (subclauses) in the system of grammar we are using:

i.	Adverbial Clause	[ACl];
ii.	Noun Clause	[NCl];
iii.	Relative Clause	[RCl];
iv.	Comparative Clause	[CCl];
v.	Prepositional Clause	[PCl].

There are three ways of recognising a subclause:

a) It is introduced by a subordinating conjunction (see further, Chapter 3 above), e.g. *If he comes, I'll phone the polis.* ('if' is the subordinating conjunction).

b) It is introduced by what is called a 'wh- element' (*who, whom, whose, what, which,* etc.) e.g. *Those whom I represent are aware of the concerns...* (*whom I represent* is the subclause).

c) It has a non-finite verb, that is a verb whose form does *not* indicate either tense or number. By themselves, verb-forms like *hoping, sung, to write,* and so on, fall into this category. Non-finite verbs by themselves may function as Predicators only in SCl's, e.g. *I saw her mother, walking along the road...* (*walking along the road* is the subclause).

Since they are embedded in a main clause or even inside a phrase, subclauses function as SPOCA elements within the main clause, or they function as modifiers inside the phrase. They also have internal SPOCA structures of their own. Thus, when you are analysing a complex sentence, you must bracket and label *all* the phrases in the sentence, e.g.

$$\text{S} \quad \text{P} \qquad \text{S} \quad \text{P} \quad \text{A}$$
$$\text{Se} \; \{ \; \text{MCl} \, [\, (...) \, (...) \; \text{SCl} \, [\, (...) \, (...) \quad (...) \,] \,] \; \}$$

Putting information into a subclause often has the effect of *downplaying* that information, i.e. making it seem less important than the information in the main clause. There is a general correlation between the level of an element in the rank scale and its importance in a sentence. Thus information conveyed inside a phrase is often of lesser importance than that in either a main clause or a subclause.

Let us now consider the five types of subclause listed above in more detail.

8.5.1 Adverbial Clauses   [ACl]

Some subclauses function in the same way as those phrases which function as Adverbials. Consider the sentence below:

```
         A x  M  H   M x   H        A   x   S  H P H  A x H
21. Se {MCl [(For  a couple  (of years)) SCl [when  (he) (was)  (at uni)]
         PP pr  d   N     PP pr  N      ACl  c  NP pn VP V  PP  pr N

  S  H  P  H   A  x    H
   (he)  (was)   (at Napier]}
  NP pn VP  V   PP  pr   N
```

This sentence has at its core the Subject and Predicator *he* + *was* and three Adverbials: *for a couple of years, when he was at uni, at Napier*. The first and third of these Adverbials are phrases – Prepositional Phrases. The second Adverbial is an embedded clause because it contains its own Subject and Predicator (*he* + *was* again) and also its own Adverbial, realised by another Prepositional Phrase: *at uni.*

In general, the Adverbial Clause has some grammatical similarities to the Prepositional Phrase. They share the grammatical property of mobility in the sentence. By moving the Prepositional Phrase and the Adverbial Clause around, we can rewrite (21), for example, as *He was, for a couple of years, at Napier, when he was at uni.* In addition, Adverbial Clauses, Adverbial Phrases and Prepositional Phrases all convey similar types of meaning, namely location in time and space, direction, manner, and so on.

These meanings in fact help us to identify several common sub-types of Adverbial Clause, ACls of *reason, manner, condition, purpose, contrast* and *place.* We can classify them according to the subordinating conjunctions that introduce them and the questions they answer. You can compare the meanings of Adverbial Clauses with those of individual adverbs.

<pre>
        S H P H C M   M   H   A   x   S H
22. Se { MCl [(He)   (is)   (very, very strong) SCl [because (he)
        NP pn VP V AjP Av   Av   Aj   ACl   c   NP pn

   P H   O H
   (plays) (rugby)...]]}
   VP V NP N
</pre>

This is an ACl of *reason*, answering the question 'Why?' Such clauses can also be introduced by the conjunctions *as* and *since*.

As noted above, ACls share with other Adverbials the property of mobility in a sentence. For example, the ACl of *manner* which occurs at the end of example (23) below can easily be switched to the beginning, as in (23a); so SPAA becomes ASPA.

```
            S M  H  P H A x  M M H   A P  H
23. Se { MCl [ (Fruit bats) (drip) (from the fig trees) SCl [ (looking)
            NP N   N VP V PP pr   d  N   N   ACl VP V

C  H
(furtive.)]]}
AjP Aj


          A  P   H   C  H    S  M H  P H
23a. Se { MCl [ SCl [ (Looking) (furtive)]   (fruit bats) (drip)
             ACl VP   V   AjP Aj    NP N  N  VP V

A  x  M M   H
(from the fig trees.)]]}
PP pr  d  N   N
```

ACls of *manner* answer the question 'How?' In this case, the ACl is introduced by a non-finite verb, *looking*. ACls can also be introduced by a range of conjunctions, such as *as, as if, so that* and *though*. An example of a similar sentence using a complex conjunction, *as if*, answers the question: 'How does the media behave?'

```
            A  x   H   S M  H   P  H      A   x
24. Se {MCl [  (In general) (the media)  (behave) SCl [ as if
            PP pr  N   NP d   N    VP V       ACl   c

S M   M    H      P  M  x  H
(the Scots language) (does not exist.)]]
NP d   N    N      VP a   n   V
```

Other ACls include those of *condition*, which are introduced by *if* or *unless*:

```
             A  x S H  P H  C  H    S H  P  M  H  O H
25. Se { MCl [ SCl [ If  (you) (are) (cold)]  (tea) (will warm) (you.)]}
             ACl  c NP pn VP V AjP Aj  NP N  VP a  V   NP pn


            S M   H    P  M x  H   A  x   M   H
26. Se { MCl [ (My parents) (needn't know) (about the psychiatrist)
            NP d   N    VP a  n  V   PP pr   d   N

A   x   S H  P  H
SCl [unless  (he)  (insists.)]]}
ACl    c  NP pn VP  V
```

ACls of *purpose*, which answer the question 'Why?', are introduced by complex (multi-word) conjunctions such as *so that* or *in order that*:

```
        S  H   P M   H    A    x    S  H P M  H    O H
27. Se {MCl [ (Men) (have died) SCl [so that (you) (can have) (jotters.) ]]}
        NP N VP a     V  ACl    c  NP pn VP a   V  NP N
```

Examples of other Adverbial Clauses are those of *contrast* –

```
         A      x      S M     H       P H
28. Se { MCl [ SCl [ Although  ( the languages )   (are)
          ACl      c    NP  d      N      VP V
```

```
 C    M      H    S  H     P H  x  C   H   M  x     H
  (closely related)]  ( Scots)  (is not) (derived (from English.))]]}
AjP  Av    Aj   NP  N   VP V   n AjP  Aj  PP   pr    N
```

– and *place*. Sentence (29) below includes an ACl of place, which answers the question 'Where?' Indeed, such clauses can be introduced by the conjunction *where* as well as conjunctions such as *wherever*:

```
        S    H        P H C M  H      A    x     S   H
29. Se { MCl [  (Accessibility)   (is)  (an issue) SCl [wherever  (people)
            NP     N        VP V NP d  N    ACl    c    NP   N
 P   H
   (go.)]]}
 VP  V
```

8.5.2 Noun Clauses

Like NPs, Noun Clauses function as S and O at clause level. They are commonly introduced by the conjunction *that*, although this is often omitted, especially in speech.

```
        S  H    P  H      O  x   S  H  P  H   C M   H
30.  Se {MCl [ (They) (knew) SCl [that  (it)  (was)  (a problem...]]}
        NP pn  VP  V   NCl   c NP pn VP V  NP d    N
```

```
               S      P     O
Compare:     MCl [ (They) (knew)  (something)].
```

The Noun Clause *that it was a problem* in the first example above fulfils the same function as the pronoun *something* in the Noun Phrase in the second example, i.e. they are both Object. An identifying feature of NCls is that they can be replaced by a pronoun.

NCls occasionally occur at S in formal language:

S
31. Se {MCl [SCl [*That it comes from Gaelic and means 'the mouth of the*
NCl

Messan, '] is not in dispute...]}

The reason why this type of sentence in rare, particularly in colloquial language, is because its Subject – *That it comes from Gaelic and means 'the mouth of the Messan'* – is rather long and therefore hard to process. Our usual preference is to put long, complex elements towards the end of the sentence where they seem to be easier to comprehend. This is known as the principle of *end weight*.

Extraposition of Noun Clauses
Sometimes, in order to preserve the principle of end weight, we use a grammatical manoeuvre to push the Subject Noun Clause to the end of the sentence, filling its usual place in the sentence with a *dummy Subject*. We saw examples of the dummy Subject *there* earlier (Chapter 7.2.1), in so-called *existential clauses* beginning with *there is/are*. In the extraposition of Noun clauses, we mark the Subject slot with the pronoun *it*, which here has no referent, and push the real Subject to the end of the sentence. So, a sentence such as –

S
32. Se {MCl [SCl [*That she had been through some very bad things*]
NCl
was obvious.]}

– is more usually found in speech in the form that it has in one of the SCOTS corpus conversations (including the hesitant repetition of the determiner *some*):

```
          S x   P H  C   H      S  x  S H
32a. Se { MCl [  (It)   (was) (obvious) SCl [ that (she)
          NP pn VP V  AjP Aj    NCl   c NP pn
```

```
   P  M    H   A    x     M
   (had been)  (through some
   VP a   V   PP   pr     d
```

```
   M   M    H     H
   (very bad) things.]]}
   AjP Av   Aj    N
```

Here note that we have analysed the dummy Subject *It* as being neither a headword nor a modifier, since it is simply a grammatical place-keeper for the proper subject of the sentence, which is *that she had been through some very bad things.*

Noun Clauses are used frequently in what is called *reported* or *indirect speech*, e.g. after a verb like *say, observe, note, complain, suggest,* etc. What is said, observed, noted, complained about or suggested is the Object of the sentence, often realised by a NCl:

```
        S H   P  H    O    x   S  H  P   H
33. Se { MCl [ (I)  (said) SCl [ that  (I)  (preferred)
        NP pn VP V   NCl   c  NP pn VP   V
```

```
   O  M    H    Co  H
   (my breakfast)  (fried.) ]]}
   NP  d   N    AjP Aj
```

8.5.3 Direct Subordination

The type of subclauses we have looked at so far – ACls and NCls – are examples of direct subordination. That is to say, the subclause is embedded one level below in the *rank scale*, which is a term sometimes given to the grammatical hierarchy that runs from *sentence, clause, phrase, word* to *morpheme*. An embedded clause can function as a constituent one rank below its normal place on the rank scale – so, for example, an embedded Noun Clause can function as the Subject of the main clause, as we saw above.

8.5.4　Indirect Subordination

Sometimes, however, subordination involves embedding clauses at even lower levels on the rank scale. This is known as *indirect subordination* or *rank shift*. Some subclauses do not function as elements embedded inside other clauses, but as elements inside other *phrases*. That is to say, they function as modifiers within phrases such as NPs:

```
      M  H    M  S  H  P  M    H   A  x  M    H
34.  (the houses   [ (that) (should be)  (in the system)])
     NP d  N  RCl NP pn VP  a     V  PP pr d    N
```

Note that, in the example above, the word *that* does not function as a conjunction but as a kind of pronoun. More details will be given on this change in function as we turn to the most common examples of indirect subordination, starting with further examples of this kind of subclause, the Relative Clause.

8.5.5　Relative Clauses

The commonest place where indirect subordination occurs is in Relative Clauses (RCl). As in example (34) above, Relative Clauses function as modifiers within phrases in much the same way as PPs. Semantically, they fulfil the function of adding information to NPs.

Thus, in example (35) below, the headword of the NP, *advisor,* is post-modified by a Prepositional Phrase and a Relative Clause in turn:

```
     M  H    M    x      H    M  S  H  P  H
35. (an advisor (within Glasgow)    [ (who) (has)
    NP d  N    PP   pr      N    RCl NP pn VP  V
```

```
O  M  H   M   x  M       H
  (a remit  (for Gaelic education))])
NP d  N  PP pr   Aj      N
```

8.5.6　Relative Pronouns and Relative Adverbs

Relative Clauses are quite easy to recognise. They are introduced by *relative pronouns*, which function as elements in the subclause (S, O). These include: *who, whom, whose, which, that.*　In the examples in the two sections immediately above, the relative pronouns, *that* and *who,* realise the Subject of the Relative Clause.

If a relative pronoun is the Subject of the Relative Clause, then, in British English at least, it is usually *included* in the sentence. If the relative pronoun is the Object, it is often omitted in colloquial language, in both Britain and North America. Compare:

```
       H    M S H   P     H       C       M                    H
36.   (heels    [ (which) (seemed) (desperately uncomfortable)])
      NP N  RCl NP pn VP   V     AjP     Av                   Aj
```

```
       H     M P     H       C       M                    H
36a.  *(heels    [ (seemed) (desperately uncomfortable)])
      NP N  RCl   VP V      AjP     Av                   Aj
```

```
            H        M O H     S   M    M    H  P M     H
37.  (opportunities [ (which)  (the public body) (will provide)
     NP        N     RCl NP pn NP  d    N     N VP a    V
```

```
A  x  M   H
   (for its staff)])
PP pr d    N
```

```
            H        M S M   M    H  P M     H     A  x  M   H
37a.  (opportunities [   (the public body) (will provide) (for its staff)])
     NP        N     RCl NP  d    N     N VP a    V    PP pr d    N
```

Example (36) above cannot be rephrased as *heels seemed desperately uncomfortable,* because the relative pronoun is the Subject of the subclause and therefore obligatory. Example (37) can be rephrased as a reduced Relative Clause, *opportunities the public body will provide for its staff,* since the relative pronoun here is the Object of the subclause, and so it is optional. In Relative Clauses like the second one, the relative pronoun can be thought of as a variant of *this* or *these* which has been moved to the front of the subclause:

> the public body will provide **these** for its staff   →
> **which** the public body will provide for its staff

Relative clauses can also be introduced by *relative adverbs*, such as *where, when, why, how.* Relative adverbs and relative pronouns together are sometimes described simply as 'wh-elements'.

```
          M  H M   A   H     S   H     P M        H
38.   (the area [    (where) (rescuers) ( were converging )])
      NP d  N RCl AvP Av     NP  N      VP a        V
```

129

```
     M  H M  A  H  S  M    H    P H    O M   H
39.  (the time [     (when)  (young lovers)  (plighted) (their troth)])
     NP d   N RCl AvP Av  NP  Aj    N    VP V    NP d   N
```

Examples (38) and (39) can be rephrased, with the Adverb phrases *when* and *where* rewritten as Prepositional Phrases that include the relative pronoun:

```
        M  H M  A x   H    S   H     P  M      H
38a.   (the area [    (in which) (rescuers) ( were converging )])
        NP d  N RCl PP pr  pn  NP   N    VP a       V
```

```
        M  H M     H  S  M    H    P H    O M   H   A x
39a.   (the time [    (that)  (young lovers) (plighted) (their troth)  (in)])
        NP d  N RCl ...pn NP  Aj   N   VP V    NP d   N   PP pr...
```

In (39a), there is a 'stranded' preposition: it should technically precede 'that', but of course we would not say *the time in that young lovers plighted their troth* – we would have to change the relative pronoun, *that,* to *which.*

Note that relative adverbs should not be confused with the conjunctions introducing Adverbial and other subclauses. A particular problem arises with *that,* a word with a great many grammatical functions. In NPs, *that* is a determiner (*that book*) and in AjPs in speech it is sometimes an adverb intensifying an adjective *(that shy).* In NCls *that* is a conjunction (*She knows that you can't*) and as a conjunction it falls outside any phrase. In RCls *that* is a pronoun, it is the headword of a NP, and so it has a clause function as S or O. In RCls – but *not* in NCls –*who(m) or which* are interchangeable with *that.*

```
       M      M    M O H   S H P   H
40.  (the members  [ (whom) ( I )  (represent)])
      NP  d   N   RCl NP  pn NP pn VP  V
```

```
       M      M    M  O H   S H P   H
40a. (the members  [  (that)  ( I )  (represent)])
      NP  d   N   RCl NP  pn NP pn VP   V
```

```
      S  H   P   M   x  H     O  x  S  H P H   C  H
41.  MCl [(we) (would not say) SCl [that (it)  (was) (wrong)]]
      NP pn VP  a    n    V    NCl c NP pn VP V  AjP Aj
```

```
          S  H  P  M  x  H      O  x  S  H  P  H   C  H
41a.  *MCl [(we)  (would not say)  SCl [who  (it)   (was)  (wrong)]]]
          NP pn  VP        a       n   V    NCl  c  NP pn VP  V  AjP  Aj
```

A distinction is often made between restrictive and non-restrictive relative clauses, which are sometimes called defining and non-defining relative clauses. Non-restrictive or non-defining relative clauses give extra, additional information about the headword, which could be deleted from the noun phrase in which the RCl occurs without any danger that the headword would not be identifiable. Restrictive or defining relative clauses specify or limit the reference of the headword that they modify. Examples from the SCOTS corpus are:

42. it was written by Dudley D. Watkins, [who was an Englishman.]
43. I've got some friends [who are Buddhists.]

In (42) the non-restrictive RCl *who was an Englishman* adds information about the headword *Dudley D. Watkins,* but it is not necessary to identify him. By contrast, the restrictive RCl in (43), *who are Buddhists*, is necessary to identify which members of the set expressed by the headword, *friends,* we are talking about. Often the punctuation provides a clue to the type of RCl that is being used: there is normally a comma between a headword and a non-restrictive RCl, while no comma separates a headword and a restrictive RCl. This punctuation convention is followed in examples (42) and (43) but it is not entirely reliable.

8.5.7   Sentential Relative Clauses

Relative clauses sometimes act as a comment on a clause or sentence, in much the same way as attitude adverbs. In such cases they function as Adverbials, because they do not post-modify a single noun; instead they *comment* on the proposition as a whole.

```
                  S  H  A    H     P  M  H     A    S  H     P  H
44.   Se { MCl [   (it)  (probably)  (will die) SCl[ (which)   (is)
                  NP pn  AvP  Av    VP  a   V    RCl NP pn  VP   V
```

```
C  M   H
   (a shame)]}
NP d    N
```

131

In the above example, *which is a shame* comments on the preceding clause *it probably will die,* as a whole, and does not refer specifically to any single word in that clause.

8.5.8 Comparative Clauses

Another place where *indirect* subordination occurs is in *Comparative Clauses* (CCl). These are quite easy to recognise because – as their name suggests – they always express some sort of comparison, but they come in a variety of different forms and are often subject to ellipsis (the omission of unnecessary words). They are usually preceded by comparative adjectives (like *older*) or adjectives modified by certain adverbs (like *more likely, more directly affected*). The CCl functions as a modifier in an Adjective Phrase:

```
         A    H    S H   P H   C H    M   x    S   H   P H
45.   MCl [ (obviously) (I)   ('m)  (older SCl [ than   (you) (are)])]
         AvP  Av  NP pn  VP V AjP Aj  CCl   c   NP  pn  VP V
```

Compare the above example with the version of it given below:

```
           S H   P H   C H    M   x    H
45a.  Se {MCl [ (I)   ('m)  (older  ( than  you ))]}
           NP pn VP V  AjP Aj  PP pr    pn
```

In (45a), the VP in the subclause has been omitted, which prompts us to interpret *than* as a preposition rather than a conjunction. The sequence *than you* therefore becomes a PP, post-modifying *taller* in a complex AjP. An alternative would be to analyse *than you* as a Comparative Clause with a missing Predicator, but some people are unhappy about analysing 'invisible' elements, so the former option is preferred here.

8.5.9 Prepositional Clauses

The fifth type of clause is the *Prepositional Clause* (PCl). These are easy to recognise because they always begin with a preposition. In this respect, they are similar in form to prepositional phrases. However, they differ from PPs in that, like all clauses, they contain a Predicator. Like PPs, PCls function as either A or M. Examples include:

```
         S   H    P   M       H
46.   MCl [ (Graves) (became intrigued)
         NP  N   VP   a       V
```

```
        A   x  O   H        S  H  P  H  CoM   M    H
SCl [ by  (something)     (he) (called) (the Black Goddess.)]]
PCl  pr NP     pn         NP pn VP V   NP d   Aj    N
```

```
        S  M  H   P H   C  M    H
47.  MCl [ ( the list)  (is)   ( a restatement
        NP d  N  VP V  NP  d    N
```

```
     M   x   S  H   P H  A   H   A  x    H
SCl [ of   (what)  (is)  (already ) (in legislation)])]
PCl  pr NP pn   VP V  AvP Av   PP  pr    N
```

Notice that example (46) exhibits direct subordination while (47) exhibits indirect subordination. That is, in (46) the PCl is embedded as an Adverbial in another clause, whilst in (47) the PCl is embedded inside a NP as a modifier. PCls are essentially Noun Clauses expanded by the addition of a preposition (in much the same way as PPs are expansions of NPs by the addition of a preposition). Note that after the preposition the very first element of the NCl can be either the Object or the Subject – in the first example above it is the Object (*Graves called **something** the Black Goddess*) while in the second example it is the Subject (***something** is already in legislation*).

This completes our brief survey of basic clause types, and gives some idea of the variety of patterns that are available in English.

8.6 Activity

By this point in the book, you should be able to identify and analyse complex sentences, that is a sentence which has at least one subordinate clause. Which of sentences 1-5 below, all taken from the SCOTS corpus, is an example of each of the following:

a) a complex sentence containing an embedded Prepositional Clause as an Adverbial Clause

b) a complex sentence containing an embedded Adverbial Clause introduced by a conjunction

c) a complex sentence containing an embedded Comparative Clause

d) a complex sentence containing an embedded Noun Clause

e) a complex sentence containing a Noun which is post-modified by a Relative Clause.

1. **What you have is an advance copy.**
2. **Upstairs were loft bedrooms, which had skylight windows.**
3. **Are you happier in Morningside than you were at the Grassmarket?**
4. **We will all take a keen interest in what is happening.**
5. **The bill has moved in that direction, although there is potential for further reform**

Now try analysing the sentences fully. They are quite tricky in places!

Chapter 9   Verb Systems

9.0   About this Chapter

This chapter takes a detailed look at the verb phrase (VP). The VP is particularly important, because at the level of clause, it functions as Predicator, and, as we have seen, the Predicator is the essential core of any major clause in English and Scots.

The VP conveys a rich complex of meanings through a variety of forms. The verb *to dance*, for example, occurs in many forms in the expressions *she dances, she danced, she is dancing, she has danced, she might have been dancing, she was dancing, she had been dancing,* not to mention *his toes had been danced upon.* This unit explores ways of understanding how these different forms express different meanings. The key concept in this exploration is that of a *system*.

9.1   Linguistic Systems

Linguistic systems are simply sets of choices – for example, the choice between saying *she dances* and *she danced.* Here there is a choice of *forms,* that is a choice between using the inflexion <-s> and the inflexion <-ed>. Making the choice changes the *meaning* of the verb in some way – here we might argue that the choice between present and past tense changes the *time of action* indicated. As we shall soon see, the relationship between tense choice and time indicated is not a simple one. There are different kinds of choices made each time we use a verb phrase in English. The range of choices is described here as a set of *simultaneous* systems – in other words, for *every* verb phrase used, different sets of choices *must* be made.

The concept of a system is important in the study of language generally, not just in grammar. As noted above, a system occurs where there is a choice of forms, i.e. where we have to choose one possibility from amongst a range of possibilities. An example of a system is the paradigm (the technical name for a table of examples) for the *present tense* verb given below. When we select from this paradigm in English, we have to match up our choice of pronoun with the *run/run-s* forms of the verb.

I run	We run
You run	You run
He, she, it runs	They run

The verb system is therefore associated with pronoun systems, which themselves contain a lot of grammatical information.

9.2   Pronoun Systems

Pronouns in English are marked for three systems, or sets of choices, namely number, gender and person:

Type of System	Available Choices
Number	(singular, plural)
Gender	(masculine, feminine, neuter)
Person	(first, second, third).

Some pronouns are also marked for *case,* that is they change their form depending on whether they are expressing the Subject or Object of the clause, or whether they are expressing possession. For example:

- he/they (*nominative case* – expressing the Subject)
- him/them (*accusative case* – expressing the Object)
- his/their (*genitive case* – expressing possession).

Other languages, and earlier forms of English, have or had further case choices, for example the *dative* case of nouns in Old English indicates that they are being used in Prepositional Phrases. Old English was the language spoken in parts of England and southern Scotland until around the middle of the 12th century.

Using these four systems (person, number, gender and case), we can write a detailed description of each pronoun, e.g. 'He' is the *third person, singular, nominative* form for the *masculine* gender. 'They' is the *third person, plural, nominative* form for *all genders*.

Now, if we choose the pronoun 'he', or the third person singular feminine or neuter nominative pronouns 'she' or 'it' as the Subject of a sentence, we must choose an appropriate verb form, like *run-s*. The systems of the verb and pronoun are thus interrelated. As we saw earlier, another way of putting this is that there must be *concord* or *agreement* between the Predicator, or VP, and its Subject, in this case the pronoun, as example (1) shows. (1a) and (1c) are acceptable standard English; (1b) is acceptable only in varieties that do not keep the concord 'rule'.

```
          S H   P H    O H
1a.   MCl [ (He)  (likes)  (them.)]
          NP  pn VP V   NP  pn


          S H    P H   O H
1b.   * MCl [ (They)  (likes)  (him.)]
          NP   pn   VP V   NP pn


          O H    S H   P H
1c.   MCl [ (Them)  (he)   (likes.)]
          NP  pn  NP pn  VP V
```

Although it is an acceptable sentence, the word order in example (1c) above is unusual, because of the fronting of the Object. The sentence begins with two NPs (*Them he*) but it remains unambiguous because the Predicator *likes* requires a singular Subject, and in this case the only option available is *he*. There is, in other words, no doubt about which NP is the Subject and which the Object because of the case of the two pronouns. In (1c) *he* is in the nominative case, and *them* in the accusative case, the cases associated with Subject and Object respectively.

In Old English, all full NPs were explicitly marked for case, which allowed word order to be more flexible than it is in Present-Day English. Hough and Corbett (2006) is an introduction to Old English, written for those with no previous experience of language study. It is recommended if you want to explore the earliest variety of the language further, and get a taste of the surviving literature. Some Scots forms, such as *hame* and *yon,* are closer than Present-Day English forms to their common ancestral roots.

In Present-Day English, words have mostly lost the case endings which gave speakers of Old English clues to their grammatical function, so we rely more on *word order* to signal grammatical functions – and so the meanings of phrases. For us today, Subjects normally occur *before* the VP, while Objects and Complements occur *after* the VP. The inflexibility of word-order in Present-Day English accounts for the apparently deviant sentence constructions in English, in which *there* and *it* function as 'dummy Subjects' – as we saw earlier in Chapter 7.2.1 – effectively marking the place of the Subject, while the important information in the sentence is shunted elsewhere:

2. **There's a <u>fancy dress shop</u> near there.**
3. **It's a shame <u>that they stopped giving kids milk</u>**

Languages other than English, many of which still have case endings, rely less on word-order, and have no need of 'dummy Subjects'. For example, Brazilian Portuguese does not use them in sentences such as the following:

4. *É pena que ele não venha.*   (Literally, *Is pity that he would not come.)
5. *Há banheiro privativo?* (Literally, *Have [= is there] private bathroom?)

9.3   The Formal Constituents of the Verb Phrase

We have already seen that the VP, in its role as Predicator, is an essential element of the clause. When making a grammatical analysis, the first step is normally to identify the Predicator(s). The VP that realises the Predicator is analysed in terms of *main verb* (V) and any *auxiliary verbs* (a). Auxiliary verbs are subdivided into primary auxiliaries (*be, have, do*) and modal auxiliaries (e.g. *can, must, should;* see further, 9.9 below).

9.3.1   Primary Auxiliaries

The forms of the verb have been developing throughout the history of English, and they continue to develop, as is particularly evident in non-standard speech. Modern English verbs can be quite complex and contain a lot of information. This is achieved through the use of *inflexional suffixes* and a range of *auxiliary verbs*. Consider the amount of information packed into the verb phrases in the following sentence, taken from the SCOTS corpus:

6. **Perhaps that *would not have dealt* entirely with Jamie Stone's perennial cheese problem, but it *might have helped* when we *were implementing* European legislation.**

In this example, the auxiliaries *would, might, have* and *were* are used in the formation of the complex VPs. These auxiliaries help position the actions realised by the main verbs in terms of actuality, possibility, time and duration. We shall shortly look in more detail at how these auxiliaries work. In the meantime, two points are worth repeating:

(a) *Every major clause must contain a main verb.* If there is only one verb in a clause, then that verb must be a main verb.

(b) *All three primary auxiliaries can act BOTH as auxiliary verbs and as main verbs.*

Compare the form and function of *be, have* and *do* in the following clauses, all again from the SCOTS corpus:

```
         S M  H    P M   H
7.    MCl [ (my mum)  (was working)]
         NP d  N   VP a    V


        S M   H   P M H
8.    MCl [ (her accent)  (has changed)]
        NP d      N   VP a  V


        S  M   H     P H  C   H
9.    MCl [ (His mother)  (was)  (Polish)]
        NP  d   N      VP V  AjP  Aj


         S   H    P H   O M M  H  A x  H
10.   MCl [ (Fiona)   (has)   (a bad side)  (to her)]
         NP   N    VP V  NP d   Aj  N PP pr pn


        S M  H   P H  O  M   M       H    A x    H
11.   MCl [ (my wife)  (did)  (her masters degree)  (at Edinburgh)]
        NP d   N   VP V  NP  d   N        N    PP pr   N
```

```
         S H  PM H  A x M   M      H   A x M M   H
12.   MCl [ (I)   (did go)  (to the Sunday School)  (for a wee while)]
      NP pn VP a  V PP pr d    N       N  PP pr d  Aj  N
```

In (7) *was* is part of the VP, modifying the main verb, while in (9) *was* is the only verb in the clause, and therefore must be the main verb, the headword. The verb *to be* here is fulfilling one of its commonest functions, that of linking the Subject to a Complement. Likewise, *has* is an auxiliary in (8) and a main verb expressing the idea of possession in (10). Some varieties of English avoid the use of *has* as a main verb expressing possession – this use is found in Scotland and in North America, but in England the main verb would usually be *got,* with *has* or *'s* as the auxiliary: *Fiona's **got** a bad side to her.* As (11) and (12) illustrate, *do* can also function as either the main verb or as an auxiliary. On the auxiliary use of *do,* see further 9.11 below.

9.4   Verb Systems

A further function of the VPs in a sequence of clauses is to show the relationship between the different events described. Consider again the three linked clauses in sentence (6) above, which is reproduced below for convenience:

6.   **Se { MCl [Perhaps that *would not have dealt* entirely with Jamie Stone's perennial cheese problem,] but MCl [it *might have helped* SCl [when we *were implementing* European legislation.]]}**

The modal auxiliary verb *would* in the first VP expresses a hypothetical situation – we know that the measures that are being discussed to solve the 'perennial cheese problem' did not in fact happen. The second VP expresses the degree of confidence the speaker has in the success of the hypothetical measures – he thinks that it is possible that they would have helped, but he is not sure. The third VP is related in time to the second – if the measures had been taken, and if they had helped, they would have helped for the duration of the implementation of the European legislation. The VPs, then, express concepts such as factuality, possibility, time and duration. In order to describe such phenomena more accurately, we need to look at the systems of the verb in more detail. Remember, 'systems' are simply sets of meaningful choices, indicated by changes in the form of the verb. There are six systems of the verb in English: *tense, aspect, voice, finiteness, modality* and *mood.* Choices from *all* of these systems must be made for every verb used in speech or writing.

9.5 Tense

In formal terms, tense is a two-part system, involving a choice between present (*I walk, I run*) and past (*I walk-ed, I ran*). The Scots system is the same, except that the past-tense marker for regular verbs in Scots is often – *t,*or *–it,* e.g. *wantit.* In English and Scots, concepts like futurity and possibility are expressed through the use of auxiliaries (see 9.9 below).

As the labels, *present tense* and *past tense,* suggest, tense is mainly, but not exclusively, used to relate the events we are talking about to *time.* In common with speakers of many other languages, we tend to envisage time as a continuous line, with the speaker occupying the point 'now'.

In many common verbs, the past tense and past participle are irregular; that is, they change form by altering the middle vowel rather than by adding *-ed*: *he ran, he has run* rather than *he walked, he has walked.* There are about 200 such verbs in Modern English, but there used to be many more. The number varies in Scots, since some irregular verbs in English (such as *told*) have become regular verbs in Scots (e.g. *telt*). This shows the force of *analogy* in language: irregular verbs tend to become regular and newer verbs tend to have regular forms, by analogy with the majority.

For example, *light* is a common irregular verb, with the past tense and past participle *lit,* as is evident from the following example from the SCOTS corpus:

13.   **The outside was *lit* by gaslamp.**

However, newer verbal compounds with *light,* such as *highlight,* tend to have regular past tenses and past participles, e.g.

14.   **We have *highlighted* three or four concerns.**

Perhaps influenced by the compound use, the SCOTS corpus does have stray incidences of *light* as a regular verb, typically in speech:

15.   **she had this earring that, like, *lighted* up?**

As suggested in the heading of this section, tense choices usually indicate the *time* of an action or event – but not always. Admittedly, the choice between present tense in *She dances **today**,* and past tense in *She danced **yesterday*** might be described as expressing present and past time. However, the situation is more complicated than it appears. What about *She dances **every day** at nine o'clock*? The tense chosen here is present tense – but the Adverbial makes it clear that the time reference is past, present *and* future.

In other words, the choice of the tense here is governed more by the question *Is this a fact?* rather than *At what time does/did this occur?* 'Factual' uses of the present tense include general statements like *The sun is the centre of our universe,* or *Water boils at 100 degrees,* or *The train leaves tomorrow morning at nine.* In the final example, the time reference is in fact the future, not the present, but the speaker's choice of the present tense indicates that s/he considers the action to be a fact, something s/he is very certain about.

Similarly, 'past' tense can sometimes be used to indicate **'distance from fact'** – that something is a possibility or a desire, as when a speaker says *Were you interested in coming on Saturday?* as a polite invitation. The use of past tense 'were' here rather than present tense 'are' distances the possibility that the listener *is* interested, and so makes the question more polite.

Politeness itself can be regarded as the negotiation of **'social distance'**. Using present tense forms of auxiliary verbs reduces 'social distance' between speakers, while using past tense forms can increase 'social distance'. What do you think the relationship of the speaker and listener is in the following requests from the SCOTS corpus: ***Please can you repair this?*** and ***Could you move on, please?*** Neither utterance, of course, refers to actions in the past.

For the reasons discussed above, making a simple correlation between *tense* and *time* should be resisted. After all, there is more to the concept of time than the matter of past, present and future. What we call the 'past tense' of a verb can as easily indicate the relationship between speakers ('social distance') and whether something is a fact or speculation ('distance from fact'), as well as past versus present (or 'distance in time').

As well as these types of 'distance', the *duration* of an event or action, and how *recently* it occurred, might also be important enough to indicate grammatically. This is not done through the system of tense, but through the system of *aspect*.

9.6   Aspect

Aspect is formally a three-part system comprising of

- simple aspect
- progressive (or continuous) aspect
- perfect (or perfective) aspect

The system of tense *combines* with the system of aspect to produce complex forms, e.g. present or past simple, present or past progressive, present or past perfect. The choice of one or a combination of these aspects subtlely changes the listener or reader's point-of-view of the events described. It does this in a variety of ways.

9.6.1   Simple Aspect

There are *no auxiliaries* in simple aspects. The infinitive, or base form of the verb, is used with the appropriate inflexions, *-s* or *-ed*, unless the verb is irregular, like *to go*:

He walk-*s*	He go*es* *(present simple aspect)*
He walk-*ed*	He *went* *(past simple aspect)*

The simple forms of the verb tend to express the action as a single, complete whole. They do not in themselves give information about the duration of the action, or even necessarily the time of its occurrence. Present simple is used to express facts and actions which occur habitually or regularly (e.g. *I go to the shops on Thursdays*), while past simple is used to express actions in the past which have been completed (e.g. *I went to the shops last night*). However, it is possible to use the present simple to express future events (e.g. *The train leaves at midnight tonight*).

Simple forms tend also to be used with *mental* or *emotional* processes in standard English: *I think that, you know that, she feels that...* etc. However, many Scottish speakers use progressive forms for at least some of these verbs, and this grammatical identity-marker can indicate that some speakers are Scottish, as in the following example from the SCOTS corpus:

16. So now I*'m thinking* that I'll need to save up a bit

There is also a clear tendency among younger speakers of English in the USA and Britain to use the progressive form rather than the simple form with the verb *love*. In 2003, Macdonald's launched *I'm lovin' it* as its first global advertising slogan. The informal, colloquial form and the use of the progressive aspect in the English version clearly target a youth audience. It is interesting to translate into English other language versions of the slogan – the first to be launched was the German *ich liebe es* ('I love it').

9.6.2 Progressive Aspect

The progressive aspect (often called the continuous aspect, and occasionally the durative aspect) is constructed with

- the auxiliary verb *to be* (e.g. *is/was/has been*) and
- the *present participle* (e.g. *walking, flying*).

Note that the *tense* of progressive aspect is indicated by the form of the auxiliary verb, *to be:*

17. He *is* going (*present progressive or continuous aspect*)

18. He *was* going   (*past progressive or continuous aspect*)

Progressive aspect indicates the speaker's perception of the relative *duration* of an event. Thus in sentence (19) below, the act of *considering* is perceived as being of longer duration than the act of *upsetting* the apple cart:

19.   **However, while *they were considering* setting up an inter-governmental conference to bring about the single market, a political event *upset* the apple cart—the collapse of the Soviet Union.**

When combined with the present tense, progressive aspect tends to express the notion of an action taking place at this very moment. The perception of duration is still involved – we assume that the action started before the present moment, and will continue for some time. Present progressive is therefore a much more likely indicator of 'now' than the present simple. Compare the two questions:

20.   Do you play squash?   (*present tense, simple aspect*)

21.   Are you playing squash now?   (*present tense, progressive aspect*)

As noted in the section above, present simple indicates a general fact, while present progressive indicates an action occurring at this moment. When the present progressive is used with an adverb like 'always', it tends to express irritation or disapproval. Compare the following two sentences from one of the SCOTS corpus texts:

22.   **She *is always crying*.**   *(present tense, progressive aspect)*

23.   **When *I cry* it is for a reason.**   *(present tense, simple aspect)*

9.6.3   Perfect Aspect

The final type of aspect, perfect or perfective, is formed with

- the auxiliary verb *have*
- followed by the *past participle* of the verb (e.g. *has wandered, have searched, will have arrived*).

The meaning of the perfect aspect is quite subtle: it is used to indicate

- events which recently occurred, relative to a point of time in the present or past, and
- events which occurred in the past, but at a time which is not specified.

The perfect aspect combines with both tense and aspect to produce complex forms and shadings of meaning.

Present perfective aspect often describes an event which was completed in the recent past. For this meaning, it is usually combined with adverbs such as 'just' or 'recently'. Thus we might say:

24.   **The first edition has just sold out.**

In (24) the action is presented as happening very recently – whether it was a few seconds ago, or five minutes, or fifteen. The actual time lapse from the point of utterance is less important than conveying the *perception* that the action happened recently. For this reason, the present perfect aspect is often used in news broadcasts, particularly at the start, to give the impression that the events described are literally 'news' – that they have just occurred. Consider these two sentences from the early part of a BBC website report (www.bbc.co.uk, accessed 30th July, 2007):

25.   US President George W Bush and UK PM Gordon Brown *have held* their first formal talks, renewing pledges to fight terrorism and seek progress in Iraq.

26.   The pair *met* at Camp David, near Washington, amid widespread interest about whether they could work together.

Here, in (25) the present perfect is used to indicate events and actions when the actual time of their occurrence is not specified beyond the fact that it probably happened quite recently. In (26) changing the aspect from perfect to simple changes the perspective on the event: it is now anchored to a particular time – even though, in this instance, the time is not actually mentioned. Nevertheless, the perspective on the events has changed.

The aspect system is slightly different in British and American English. Whereas in British English, it is unacceptable, say, to use the past simple to make statements and ask questions about events which happened in the non-specific past, it is perfectly acceptable to do so in American English. Thus we have:

American English		*British English*	
27.	Did you go yet?	29.	Have you gone yet?
28.	I already did that.	30.	I've already done that.

When perfect aspect is combined with the progressive aspect as well as with tense, the notion of duration further complicates the meanings described above. For example, in (31) below, we know (i) that the action took place in the past, (ii) that it started before some given point in the past, and (iii) it lasted for some time.

31.   **Sandy had been playing outside**   *(past perfect progressive).*

Tense and aspect together, then, express key features of the speaker or writer's stance towards the events or actions being described. By selecting from the systems of tense and aspect, the speaker can give nuanced information about the proximity or distance in time of the occurrence, whether it is a general fact or an event of limited duration, and so on. The choices of tense and aspect are simultaneous, and so in some grammar books the concepts are merged, and the authors write, for example, of the 'present simple tense' or 'the present perfect tense'. However, by considering these two verb systems separately, we can see more clearly how each makes its contribution to the meaning of any verbal expression.

9.7   Voice

Voice is a two-part system, involving a choice between *active* and *passive*. Only transitive verbs (those which can be followed by an Object) occur in the passive. Note that you cannot transform (32) into the passive (i.e. you cannot say *fairly well was slept by us*):

```
        S H    P H   A M   H
32. MCl [ (We)  (slept)  (fairly well.)]              slept = intransitive verb
        NP pn  VP V AvP Av  Av
```

```
       A     H      S H    P H  O H    A x  M H     Active voice:
33. MCl [(Afterwards) (people) (gave) (alms)  (to the poor.)]   give =
       AvP   Av    NP N  VP V NP N  PP pr  d  N    transitive vb
```

```
      A       H      S H   P M   H     A x  M H    Passive voice:
33a. MCl [ (Afterwards) (alms)  (were given)  (to the poor.)]   give =
        AvP     Av    NP N  VP  a    V   PP pr d   N    transitive vb
```

In what is sometimes called the *passive transformation,* the Object of an active sentence such as (33), here *alms,* becomes the Subject of the passive sentence (33a). The Subject of the active sentence (33), here *people,* is either omitted in the passive transformation, as in (33a), or it could be transformed into a prepositional phrase (*by people*).

There is seldom, if ever, an equal choice in a language between two members of a system that appear to communicate the same information. The active and passive voice seem to be communicating identical information, but in fact the choice between active and passive voice can be important in stylistic terms. Consider the different effects of the following:

34.   *It has been drawn* to our attention that foodstuffs *are being consumed* in the lecture room.

34a.   *Somebody told* me that *people are eating* during lectures.

(34) uses the passive voice in the two italicised parts, and sounds more formal than (34a). (34) might occur on an official notice, while (34a) is more likely in spoken use. The choice between active and passive can therefore be used to distinguish between formal and informal contexts of language use.

Furthermore, in the following imaginary newspaper headlines, a different emphasis is placed on elements of the clauses by the choice between active and passive:

35.   TROOPS *KILL* TWO DEMONSTRATORS
35a. TWO DEMONSTRATORS *ARE KILLED BY TROOPS*
35b. TWO DEMONSTRATORS *ARE KILLED*

In the passive sentences, (35a) and (35b), the writer also has a choice of whether to include or omit the agent. The choices made here can be ideologically significant. In (35) the headline is about the troops, and what they have done. (35a) focuses more on the demonstrators, and what has happened to them. The agency of the troops is maintained, and is presented as new information, at the end of the sentence. (35b) is again about the demonstrators and what has happened to them, but the agency of the troops is omitted.

Newspaper editors who wish to slant the information in different ways might opt for different choices here. An editor who wished to focus on the troops and on their responsibility for the killing might choose (35). An editor who wished to focus on the demonstrators, but who also wished to draw attention to the troops' involvement, might opt for (35a). Another editor, who wished to focus on the demonstrators, but also to downplay the troops' involvement, might prefer (35b). All three sentences give very similar information, but the option of choosing between active and passive can shade meanings in subtle ways. In particular, the responsibility for the actions presented can be negotiated by choosing either active or passive from the system of voice.

9.8   Finiteness

Finiteness is formally another **two-part** system. Verbs are either *finite* or *non-finite*. A finite verb can take a Subject and shows number and tense.

36.   **he (*plays*) the fiddle**   The V is finite; 3rd person
          VP   singular present tense

36b. **Robby (*is playing*) the penny whistle**   The VP is finite. The
          VP   auxiliary *is* marks the tense.

Within the VP in (36b), the finite constituent is actually the auxiliary (*is*), which shows concord with the Subject (singular), and indicates the tense (present). If number and/or tense were to change, the auxiliary would change accordingly, but the participle would remain the same (*are/was playing*). In a complex verb, the first part is **always** the finite part. The other parts are non-finite:

36c. *He (playing)
  VP

Participles by themselves are non-finite.

36d. *He (to play)
  VP

The infinitive (*to play*) is non-finite

Modal auxiliaries (see further, section 9.9 below) are followed by the infinitive (usually minus the particle, *to*). Thus in 'I can swim' and 'He should leave', *swim* and *leave* are infinitives. (Compare 'I am able *to swim*' and 'he ought *to leave*', where the infinitive is marked by 'to'.)

In prescriptive grammars, the general rule is that full and proper sentences should contain at least one finite VP. However, particularly in literary texts, sentences that have non-finite participles – or no verb at all – are frequently used to express states and processes. These grammatical choices give a timeless, 'stream of consciousness' effect to the prose, as is shown by the following excerpt from Meaghan Delahunt's novel *In the Blue House* (Bloomsbury, 2001, p. 13):

37.   And how I looked. Colour, sound and form. All my senses **engaged**.
    Entering Veracruz – the stun of those first sights – a wall of heat and drizzle; the heavy scents of coffee and vanilla. And as I stepped from sea to land, at the same point where Cortes arrived centuries before me, there was the illusion of stepping from something fluid to something more solid. The earthiness of colour and heat and scent. **Beguiled**, as the Spanish had been.

The non-finite past participles (*engaged, beguiled*) express states, while *entering* communicates a sense of process. None of these non-finite verbs is anchored to a finite auxiliary and so each happens 'out of time', giving a sense of immediacy to the passage. In addition, the many isolated NPs – *colour, sound and form, the stun of those first sights, a wall of heat and drizzle, etc.* – express a sequence of discrete sense impressions. The manipulation of finiteness, then, allows us the option of anchoring our discourse in specific time, or of letting it float free and timeless.

Like tense and aspect, voice and finiteness describe choices that are made simultaneously every time we utter or write a verb phrase. Whereas tense and aspect mainly indicate time and duration, the system of finiteness asks a broader question about whether or not an event or state can be anchored in time at all. Additionally, the system of voice allows the speaker or writer to express agency explicitly, or leave the responsibility for the action or event unsaid.

9.9 Modality

One of the most interesting and varied systems of the verb is *modality*. Like voice and tense, modality is a two-part system, consisting of *modalised* and *non-modalised* verbs. Non-modalised verbs are employed in statements and questions of fact, such as:

38a. She answered the phone.	38c. Did she answer the phone?
38b. She didn't answer it.	38d. Didn't she answer it?

Non-modalised verb phrases can be either positive or negative, but statements containing non-modalised verbs tend to share a sense of certainty – the speaker states that someone did or didn't do something. Modalised verb phrases do not share this sense of certainty. Modal auxiliary verbs are used to express the speaker's opinion about the events described in the sentence. In other words, the speaker expresses how certain he or she is that the events actually happened. In some cases, the speaker uses modality to express a sense of obligation that the events should or must occur. Occasionally, a modal auxiliary form will be used to express desirability, e.g. *May you both be very happy.* (In the past, a separate system, mood, expressed these kinds of meaning through one of three options, the subjunctive, but modality is gradually replacing the subjunctive mood in English – see further below, section 9.10.)

There are nine core modal auxiliaries: *can, could, may, might, must, shall, should, will, would.* Some grammarians also include forms like *ought to, dare,* and *need* among the modals.

9.9.1 Degrees of Certainty

The only events we can be certain about are the events that are happening around us (the present) and events that we know have already taken place (the past). In English, we use the modal auxiliary *will/shall* to refer to events in the future, i.e. when we are making a prediction about an event. (We can also refer to the future by using a present tense, often reinforced by an adverb, or *going to*, which expresses an intention.) We use auxiliaries like *can, could* to express an opinion about the lesser likelihood of something happening. Some examples are given below (modal auxiliaries are shown in *italics*).

39. The minister is telling the Parliament an untruth.
                              (Non-modalised: fact)
40. I'm going to tell my mammy about you.
                              (Non-modalised: intention)
41. I'*ll* tell you what happened.

                              (Modalised: offer or prediction)
42. you *can* tell me this story.

                              (Modalised: strong possibility)
43. maybe you *could* tell me a bit about that.

                              (Modalised: weak possibility)

In addition, certainty can be expressed as a strong deduction, using the modal auxiliary verb *must,* as in:

44. 'Oh, you *must* be frozen!' says Mummy.
                              (Modalised: deduction)

9.9.2   Permission, Advice and Obligation

Other modals are used to express social opinions, often with the implication that the speaker has some right to advise or command the listener, as in

45.   Ms Sturgeon, you may continue.
                              (Modalised: permission)
46.   You *ought to* clean your seat after your tea.
                              (Modalised: social obligation)
47.   You *should* be at school

                              (Modalised: weak obligation)
48.   You *must* never play with my lighter again

                              (Modalised: strong obligation)

Those grammarians who are keen on technical terms derived from Greek sometimes refer to the modals which express possibility as *epistemic,* while modals which express obligation are *deontic.*   The basic point about modalised sentences, however, is that a range of meanings about possibility, obligation and desirability can be expressed by opting to use modal auxiliaries.

9.9.3   Variation in Modal Use

The distribution of modal auxiliaries in speech and writing is another area where Scottish and English speech habits diverge. According to the research literature, Scottish speakers are supposed to avoid obligation modals like *must,* and *ought to,* preferring *have to.* They also avoid using *may/might* to express permission, preferring *can.* There is some support for this from the written and spoken SCOTS documents, though there are issues about how representative the SCOTS texts are – even at 4 million words the corpus is quite small. However, the frequency of modal uses in the SCOTS data at the time of writing is roughly as follows:

Modal auxiliary verb	Total Number in SCOTS	Number in Spoken Docs only
must	2217	313
ought to	60	5
have to	1474	579
may	2996	79
might	2008	350
can	8246	2895
could	4069	950

These figures are approximate for the simple reason that searches for *may* will include the name of the month – and any women called May – and searches for *can* will include the container as well as the auxiliary verb. *Might* will also include its uses as a noun, as in *might is never right.* However, the results are still suggestive. Scottish speakers use the full range of modals listed above, but *have to* occurs more frequently in speech than *ought to* does in speech and writing combined, and *have to* occurs much more frequently than *must.* The most frequent modals seem to be *can* and *could,* and while *may* occurs frequently in writing, it is much less frequent in speech. Despite their approximate nature, the SCOTS corpus findings suggest that the research literature is generally correct. However, much more detailed research remains to be done on modal auxiliary usage in different varieties of English and Scots.

In some parts of Scotland, you can also still hear *double modal* usage – a feature that is taboo in standard English. For example, *future possibility* in Scottish English is sometimes expressed through *will+can.* There is evidence for this usage in the SCOTS corpus, at least in the written texts, mostly literary, where there are around 19 examples, e.g.

49.   **we'll can win throu**   *Isolde's Luve-Daith*

50.   **wha*'ll can* guide them**   *The Nine Sangs*

In standard English usage, modals can be combined with the systems of tense and aspect to produce subtle and complex meanings, e.g.:

51.   **They *will have had to* try to continue funding it**

Sentence (51) is a modalised perfective. The modal auxiliary *will* expresses the speaker's certainty, here, rather than futurity, and the perfect *have* indicates the recent or unspecified past. The modal auxiliary *had to* expresses past obligation. As a whole, the clause indicates that the speaker is sure that the people concerned were constrained to try to continue funding something, at some unspecified point in the past.

If you analyse the complex verb forms in standard English you will observe that their component parts generally occur in a fixed order:

Modal Auxiliary + Perfect Auxiliary + Progressive Auxiliary + Passive + Main Verb.

This fixed sequence is evident in complex verb phrases, such as are found in (52) and (53):

52.   **we *could have been goin* up to Shetland**   *(active)*

53.   **no action *could have been taken* by the Scottish ministers**   *(passive)*

9.10   Mood

The modal auxiliaries also contribute to the realisation of *mood*, which is a three-part system that is gradually becoming a two-part system. The two surviving moods are indicative and imperative; the subjunctive mood in English is gradually disappearing.

Indicative Mood
The indicative is the mood of sentences in the past or present, ie. those stating *facts*, e.g.

54.   **Independent studies *show* that reducing tobacco consumption in countries like Scotland actually increases employment overall and benefits the economy as a whole.**

Imperative Mood
The imperative is the mood of *commands*, e.g. 'Go!' Note that Predicators in the imperative mood generally have no Subject.

Subjunctive Mood

The subjunctive mood has virtually died out in contemporary English. This mood used to express desirability or hypothetical speculations, and was realised by the presence or absence of verb inflexions. Nowadays, these meanings are usually realised through the system of modality – and the use of modal auxiliaries – rather than by verb inflexions. However, a few subjunctive forms remain as fossils in the language, as in 'God bless our native land!' where the absence of the *–(e)s* inflexion in the third person singular present indicates an old subjunctive form, here expressing desirability. Such forms were quite common in Shakespeare's time, but have since been gradually replaced by modals, e.g. 'Long *may* she *live!*' rather than 'Long *live* the Queen!'. However, subjunctives are still sometimes used in *conditional* clauses introduced by conjunctions such as *if*. The variability of the mood system is shown in the following examples, (54)-(57):

55.   **I'd keep out of their clutches if I *were* you.**

56.   **If only I *were* far away frae here**.

57.   **If only I *was* (*were?*) Holden Caulfield!**

58.   **she'd do the same for me, if I *was* in her shoes**

These examples show the gradual shift in subjunctive usage. *Were* in such contexts may look like a third person plural form, but it is, in fact, a subjunctive, here expressing advice and desirability (or, indeed, wishful thinking!). Subjunctives are used in situations where facts are not being expressed – instead, desires, hypotheses, or wishes are being articulated. (55) and (56) show the subjunctive form; (57) shows that the writer is undecided about which form to use; and (58) shows the indicative form, with the hypothetical nature of the clause simply signalled by the subordinating conjunction, *if*.

The case of the disappearing subjunctive tells us something interesting about grammatical change. The *meanings* signalled by the subjunctive forms of the verb do not disappear, and so other grammatical resources must be deployed to signal things like desirability, speculation, wishes, etc. We now signal these meanings mainly through the system of modality – i.e. through modal auxiliary verbs – as well as through conjunctions like *if* and indeed through vocabulary items such as *wish, intend,* etc.

9.11   The Auxiliary 'Do'

A curiosity of the form of the VP in English is the use of *do*. *Do* is sometimes referred to as a 'dummy' element since its main function is the purely grammatical one of marking the VP in interrogative and negative clauses. Such marking is necessary only where the VP is in the simple aspect. In the other aspects, progressive and perfective, the auxiliary verbs (*is, has,* etc.) do the job of marking questions and negatives. Compare:

Progressive
59. He is sleeping.
60. He *is not* sleeping.
61. *Is* he sleeping?

Perfective
62. He had arrived.
63. He *had not* arrived.
64. *Had* he arrived?

Simple
65. He smiled.
66. He *didn't* smile. (* He smiled not.)
67. *Did* he smile? (* Smiled he?)

In examples (66) and (67), *did* fills the slot filled by the auxiliary *is* in (60) and (61) and and *has* in (63) and (64). The asterisked forms alongside (66) and (67) were perfectly acceptable at earlier stages of the language; you will find many examples of such structures in Shakespeare's writing. However, these usages declined in popularity in the modern age.

Dummy *do* is also used in short answers, as in (68) and (69), as well as in *tag questions*, such as (70) and (71), which invite the listener's agreement:

68. *Did* he go? Yes, he *did*.
69. Who cares? I *do*/His mother *does*.

70. It *was* raining hard, *wasn't* it?
71. He went, *didn't* he?

As the SCOTS corpus shows, Scottish and English speech patterns are distinguished by a different order of elements in tag questions. Whereas English tag questions generally are ordered *auxiliary + negative + pronoun,* Scottish tag questions often have the form *auxiliary + pronoun + negative,* as in the following example:

72. **Individuals lobby, do they not?**

Finally, *do* also has an emphatic function, marked by underlining or highlighting in some forms of written English:

73.   Reading <u>does</u> take up a lot of time.

9.12   Activities

Activity 1
It should be obvious by now that the VP in English is a complex phenomenon which needs a range of terms for its description. Say as much as you can about the numbered and highlighted VP's in the passage.

Example: FELL, main verb, third person singular, past simple indicative, intransitive

Abandoning his bicycle, which fell before a servant **(1) could** catch it, the young man **(2) sprang** up onto the veranda. He **(3) was** all animation.
'Hamidullah, Hamidullah! Am I late?' he cried.
(4)'Do not apologize,' said his host. 'You **(5) are** always late.'
'Kindly answer my question. Am I late? **(6) Has Mahmoud Ali eaten** all the food? If so I **(7) go** elsewhere. Mr Mahmoud Ali, how are you?'
'Thank you, Dr Aziz, I **(8) am dying.'**
'Dying before your dinner? Oh, poor Mahmoud Ali!'
'Hamidullah here is actually dead. He passed away just as you **(9) rode up** on your bike.' (lines omitted)
'Aziz, don't chatter. We **(10) are having** a very sad talk.'

E.M. Forster, *A Passage to India*, chapter 2.

Activity 2
Make a complete form and function analysis of the sentences below. All contain different types of VP structure.

a.   **Jane was talking about her Wishaw childhood.**
b.   **A tall tree twinkled its Christmas message over the statues.**
c.   **However, this has made me a sceptic.**
d.   **A concomitant impact on that will be a switch to imported tobacco.**
e.   **They must have been delivered.**

Activity 3
The following sentences might be spoken or written by a learner of English as a Foreign Language. Imagine that you are an EFL teacher. Judge whether or not the sentences are acceptable English. If they are not, how would you

explain to the learner where the error lies? (You can assume that the learner has a competent knowledge of grammatical concepts!)

1. I have met Graham on Saturday.
2. Did you see her already?
3. He's watching television every morning.
4. My neighbour always play the stereo very loudly.
5. He smoked a cigarette when I was coming in.

Activity 4

Your imaginary learner of English now brings you a list of sentences, and asks you to explain the difference in meaning between them. How do you do that? Are any of the sentences unacceptable English? Do any of the sentences have more than one possible meaning?

1. The train leaves on Saturday at noon.
2. The train is leaving on Saturday at noon.

3. The train will leave on Saturday at noon.
4. The train is going to leave on Saturday at noon.

5. The train must leave on Saturday at noon.
6. The train must be leaving on Saturday at noon.

7. The train can leave on Saturday at noon.
8. The train could leave on Saturday at noon.

9. The train left on Saturday at noon.
10. The train has left on Saturday at noon.

Activity 5   No future?

It is sometimes said that English is a language which has got no future tense – the form of the verb does not change to express futurity, as happens in other languages. How many ways can you think of to describe future states and actions in English?

Activity 6

Give a brief description, with at least TWO examples, of the verb systems of English listed below:

aspect   finiteness   mood   modality   voice

For example:

157

Question: Describe the *tense* system in English:

Model Answer:

The *tense* system in English is a two-part system involving a choice between *present* and *past*. Changes in tense are normally indicated by the inflexion '-ed' or a change in the vowel of the root verb, e.g. 'swim/swam'.

Examples of the present tense are 'I walk' and 'I run', and examples of the past tense are 'I walked' and 'I ran'.

Chapter 10 Grammar and Close Reading

10.0   About this Chapter

Through changes in curricula and passing educational fashions, 'close reading' has remained a durable component of English teaching and assessment. This chapter focuses on the role of grammatical analysis in close reading, with a particular focus on how grammatical knowledge is assessed in the close reading section of the current Scottish Qualification Authority's 'Higher' English examination. The chapter is intended to give guidance specifically to teachers and senior pupils who are teaching and learning English for the SQA 'Higher'. Other readers may find it useful to reflect on how the knowledge and skills outlined in earlier chapters can be formally assessed in English courses at secondary school or college level, and in the early years of undergraduate study.

Information about the current place of close reading in university and school curricula can be found at the following websites:

- www.qaa.ac.uk/academicinfrastructure/benchmark/statements/English07.asp
- www.ltscotland.org.uk/curriculumforexcellence/languages/literacyandenglish/index.asp

References below to the university Subject Benchmark statements and the school *Curriculum for Excellence* guidelines are taken from documents to be found on these websites.

10.1   What is 'Close Reading'?

'Close reading' is used to cover a set of highly developed reading skills that can be broken down in a number of ways. For example, close reading may involve readers paying attention to and being able to articulate interpretations based on the following textual features:

- vocabulary patterns, or the use of evocative words and phrases
- 'figures of speech', such as metaphor or simile
- grammatical patterns that may indicate a writer's particular stance, or characterise his or her individual style.

Close reading, then, involves readers in two types of activity: description and interpretation. Close readers require the technical apparatus to identify and describe patterns of vocabulary and grammar. They must also gain experience in using these patterns as a basis for making plausible claims about why the text is written as it is. It is therefore not surprising that close reading is mentioned in curricular guidance that informs course design in Scottish universities and schools.

At university level, the first of the 'key subject-specific skills' in the Subject Benchmark statements for the discipline of English (p.4) is:

- critical skills in the close reading and analysis of texts.

At school level, the *Curriculum for Excellence: Literacy and English: Principles and Practice* document (p.3), also associates close reading with 'critical literacy':

> Children and young people not only need to be able to read for information: they also need to be able to work out what trust they should place on the information and to identify when and how people are aiming to persuade or influence them.

Although the actual expression 'close reading' is absent from the *Principles and Practice* guidelines, it appears in the *Experiences and Outcomes* document (p.10). This document grades different reading levels, with respect to the pupils' developing skills in:

> investigating and/or appreciating fiction and non-fiction texts with increasingly complex ideas, structures and specialist vocabulary for different purposes.

These skills are expressed as 'can do's', the fourth and most complex level of which suggests the following:

To show my understanding, I can give detailed, evaluative comments, with evidence, on the content and form of short and extended texts, and respond to different kinds of questions and other types of close reading tasks.

The *Curriculum for Excellence* envisions grammatical knowledge, then, as a 'tool', first for fluent reading and then for the close reading of increasingly complex, increasingly unfamiliar texts.

The 'Close Reading' section of past SQA 'Higher' examinations has generally presented two related journalistic feature articles or, occasionally, extracts from non-fictional prose so that candidates can compare two different approaches to a similar theme. The comparison of texts can be a powerful learning strategy, since it may point up decisions made by individual writers about:

- the selection of content, and
- the ways that the content is presented to readers.

Very often the texts used in past SQA examinations are not Scottish in provenance – sources have included *The Times, Time* magazine, *The Economist, The Guardian* and *The Observer* – but sometimes they are. Of the Scottish texts, *The Herald* has been a frequent source of opinion, editorial or feature articles. Whatever their geographical origin, most of the sources are from the 'quality' or 'broadsheet' press, although tabloids are occasionally used or adapted. At the time of writing, the SQA 'Higher' Arrangement Documents give little specific guidance on what linguistic features might be assessed in the examination, but they do give some general guidance on the kind of texts preferred:

> A quality newspaper is likely to yield suitable material for summative purposes. At this level the internal structure of the article should be noticeably complex. It is likely that the *sentence length will be varied* for effect and emphasis. It is also likely that journalistic writing suitable for summative purposes will be characterised by a *stylistic richness*. There may indeed be an intentional discrepancy between a chosen style and the ostensible purpose of the writing: the writer may choose, for instance, to insert *colloquialisms into a formal context* to highlight the point being made. Overall scrutiny of the text may well reveal a sustained but subtle attempt to *manipulate the reader's response* through irony, humour and other devices.
> (http://www.sqa.org.uk/files/nq/English_Higher.pdf, accessed 15/04/08)

It is clear from this excerpt that any description of linguistic structure should, understandably, support an interpretation of the writer's persuasive purpose in the article. However, it also follows that in order to interpret a linguistic structure, one must first be able to describe it. The following sections consider what kind of language descriptions have been expected in previous examinations.

10.2   Paying Attention to Vocabulary

Close reading, of course, is not just about grammar – issues such as selection of vocabulary and use of punctuation are also relevant. Sophisticated close readers will consider the sources of the texts used in the examinations since, obviously, the original articles addressed different communities of readers, audiences that vary according to nation, class, and even (depending on the publication and the article) professional status and gender. The textual differences between articles directed at these different audiences might be very slight, almost indiscernible at a glance. Yet close reading pays attention to such decisions as the ones to use the word *humankind* and the phrase *hip boots* in the extract below, from a *Time* magazine article on the changes required to avoid climatic catastrophes such as global warming (from the SQA 'Higher' specimen paper, 2003):

> Only an optimist, though, and an uninformed optimist at that, could believe that *humankind* will succeed in making such radical changes in time to avert the bad weather ahead. So the best advice is to get out the umbrellas and *hip boots* and head for high ground.

There are various vocabulary items that could be used to convey the sense of *humankind,* for example, *mankind,* or even *people.* The word *mankind* is, of course, arguably marked as masculine, and as such has become an expression avoided by writers with a particular stance on gender inclusion and exclusion. *People,* on the other hand, is a more everyday term that does not necessarily communicate the idea that our entire species might have a special responsibility for environmental protection. So a close reader of this text might argue that the term *humankind* conveys a sense of 'species-hood' that includes both males and females.

The phrase *hip boots* is another matter. The expression is fairly transparent in meaning; it clearly refers to waterproof boots that reach to the hips. And yet the presence of the phrase in this text is perhaps an indication of its American origins: the phrase *hip boots* occurs 37 times in the 360 million plus Corpus of Contemporary American English, and not once in the 100 million words of the British National Corpus (these figures can be compared online at http://www.americancorpus.org/ and http://corpus.byu.edu/bnc/).

Although corpus statistics must always be approached with caution, it is clear from the American figures that the majority of usages are from magazines and newspapers, which also figure prominently in the BNC. One might also argue that behind the expression *head for the high ground* lies the more familiar idiom *head for the hills,* which again seems slightly more American than British, with only 8 appearances in the BNC against 46 in a corpus that is only three to four times larger. In conjunction, then, *hip boots* and *head for the higher ground* both suggest that the primarily American readership for this article impacts upon the choice of vocabulary.

10.3   Paying Attention to Grammar

More pertinent to this book, however, is grammatical patterning. What *grammatical* issues are close readers expected to be aware of? In past SQA 'Higher' examinations, questions on grammar tend to manage to be both specific, about the part of the texts to analyse, and vague, about what candidates are required to do with them. This book has shown that there are many aspects of grammar that *could* be commented on; the difficulty for teacher and candidate is distilling from all this information those pieces of knowledge that are relevant to any examination question. The comments in the following section are based on a sample taken from the 'Close Reading' section of SQA 'Higher' papers and specimen papers from 2003-6 (plus the recommended answers). While the 'Higher' is under review, it seems unlikely from the *Curriculum for Excellence* documents that any radical shift in the treatment of grammar and reading is planned, and so the comments are likely to be of value for the foreseeable future.

It is unsatisfactory, and indeed unfair, to try to reconstruct an approach to teaching grammar and close reading from the published answers to past examination questions. Anyone who attempts such a reconstruction would no doubt quickly characterise the approach as unsystematic, vague and often contradictory. A survey of the questions asked in 2003-6 suggests that issues of punctuation are too readily conflated with grammar; the expression 'tone' is so extended and abused as to become meaningless; and grammatical features are plucked out of the text in a random fashion while interesting rhetorical characteristics in the texts languish unnoticed. In general, close reading questions spotlight grammar at the levels of word, clause and discourse. Phrase level is curiously neglected, though much could be said about it. Often the guidance given in published answers suggests that a grammatical structure 'emphasises' content, although it might be argued that it simply expresses it. A consequence of such vague guidance is that pupils may use 'emphasis' as an all-purpose answer to questions about the impact of a grammatical usage – and it would be difficult to gainsay them. Such reservations notwithstanding, on the basis of the sample of past papers, the following list identifies those grammatical features that SQA exam setters and markers have focused on. (In the quotations from the examination texts, the original line references are given, to help those who wish to refer to the full examination paper. The source of these quotations is listed in the bibliography; see Scottish Qualifications Authority, 2006.)

10.3.1 At the Level of Words

Some past examination questions have focused on grammatical items such as determiners and pronouns. Exam questions have raised issues such as the inclusiveness or exclusiveness of determiners (*my/our, your, his/her/its/their*) and pronouns (*I/me/we/us, you, he/him/she/her/it//they/them*) to include or exclude author and/or readers in an argument. For example, the following passage from *The Herald,* written by Ruth Wishart, and featured in the 2003 'Higher', sets up clear categories of 'us' and 'them':

> Yet Ireland has managed to attract *its* young
> entrepreneurs back to help drive a burgeoning
> economy. *We* must try to do likewise. *We* need
> immigrants. *We* cannot grow the necessary skills   105
> fast enough to fill the gap sites. *We* need people
> with energy and commitment and motivation,
> three characteristics commonly found among *those*
> *whose* circumstances prompt *them* to make huge
> sacrifices to find a new life.

Here, the issue is who is being described as 'us' (presumably 'indigenous' Scots) and who is being categorised as 'them' (here, in turn, the Irish and immigrants to Scotland). The grammatical resources of determiner and pronoun construct social groups that can then be contrasted in ways that suit the writer's purpose. There is no 'natural' category that the determiners and pronouns may refer to – 'us' could in principle incorporate Europeans, or even every member of the human race or of life on Earth, so long as it is contrasted with an equally constructed 'other'.

Other exams focus on the use of particular verbs, modal auxiliary verbs, adjectives and adverbs to express possibility or obligation. The article by Ruth Wishart can again be used as an illustration:

> Yet Ireland *has managed* to attract its young
> entrepreneurs back to help drive a burgeoning
> economy. We *must try* to do likewise. We *need*
> immigrants. We *cannot grow* the necessary skills   105
> fast enough to fill the gap sites. We *need* people
> with energy and commitment and motivation,
> three characteristics commonly found among those
> whose circumstances prompt them to make huge
> sacrifices to find a new life.

Here there is a contrast between fact ('Ireland has managed...') and obligation ('We must...'), requirement ('We need...') and inability ('We cannot...'). Fact, obligation, requirement and ability are all expressed by verbs, often modal auxiliaries ('must/cannot').

As we suggested in Chapter 9 of this book, it is worth paying attention to verbs and their forms. Exam questions have probed the use of shifts in verb tense to indicate changing perspectives – to distance or bring dramatically closer. An extract from the 2006 'Higher' examination, taken from *The Economist,* illustrates a simple shift from distanced past to a more immediate present:

> When the world *was* a simpler place, the
> rich *were* fat, the poor *were* thin, and
> right-thinking people *worried* about
> how to feed the hungry. Now, in much of
> the world, the rich *are* thin, the poor *are*   5
> fat, and right-thinking people *are*
> *worrying* about obesity.

To sum up, at the level of word, examiners of close reading have been concerned with issues such as how grammatical choices at word level have established social categories. Critical, close readers should therefore be conscious of how the patterning of determiners, pronouns and nouns expresses categories such as *these/those people, us / them, Scots/ immigrants, foreigners / asylum seekers*. As noted above, these categories are questionable and can be deconstructed.

Examiners have also been interested in how verb forms articulate fact, obligation, necessity, requirement – and social and temporal immediacy and distance. In journalistic editorials and, more recently, blogs, arguments often move from a series of statements offered as facts (e.g. 'the rich *are* thin and the poor *are* fat') to a conclusion that states an obligation or necessity ('parents *should pay* more attention to children's diet'; 'food suppliers *must give* more information on labels'). Close readers, therefore, may be advised to pay particular attention to tense and modality when considering the construction of persuasive prose.

10.3.2 At Clause Level

Past examination questions and the model answers suggest that examiners are interested in two or three recurring issues at the level of the clause. The first issue is to do with the complexity of sentences. Close readers should assess the impact of writing prose that is made up largely of simple and compound sentences (i.e. sentences containing one verb phrase, and clauses strung together using the conjunctions *and, but* and *or*), or prose that is made up largely of complex sentences (i.e. sentences containing multiple subordinate, or embedded clauses).

Choosing a simple or complex sentence structure can have a number of effects. A relatively simple sentence structure is associated with speech while a relatively complex sentence structure is associated with writing. The use of 'spoken' features also reduces social distance between writer and reader and the grammatical features associated with speech may further indicate 'plain common sense'. Simple sentences also contain fewer ideas – usually one proposition per sentence – and so arguments that use simple sentences can seem 'blunt'. Another text taken from the 2006 examination paper, this time written by Susie Orbach, a clinician, for *The Observer,* illustrates a relatively simple style. The simple sentences are here italicised:

So sections of the market aim to profit   45
from the notion that we are all too fat.
We need to contest that. It isn't the case.
Evidence from the professional
journals shows that fitness, not fat,
determines our mortality. *You can be*   50
fat, fit and healthy.

A simple prose style can be contrasted with the relative sophistication of a style that deploys complex sentences, in which ideas are often linked by conjunctions that indicate their status as condition, qualification, reason, result, and so on. A complex style demands more processing by the reader, and it is more typical of ornate or philosophical prose than everyday journalism. In the following extract from *The Times,* taken from the specimen paper for the 2003 'Higher' examination, the author uses a fairly complex style – but softens it by breaking up the subordinate clauses into 'sentence fragments' (here italicised), and using tag questions and colloquial vocabulary to reduce the distance between writer and reader:

Now	40

it seems that global warming is recreating the very

same conditions which caused it to stall before,

with the potential to plunge the whole of northern

Europe into another Ice Age.

Which is a bit ironic as we slosh around in sodden,	*45*

rainswept towns and villages; as we discuss the

extraordinary late autumn and give up hope for a

white Christmas. Global warming was going to

bring Mediterranean holiday weather to Brighton

and vineyards to Argyll, wasn't it? Global	50

warming is the reason why spring-flowering iris

and cistus are blooming crazily in November. So

how could it turn England's green and rather tepid

land into a frozen waste?

Here, the use of the interrogative mood (in the tag question *wasn't it?*, and the rhetorical question that concludes the extract) can be viewed as involvement strategies that offset the complexity of the sentence structure, as evident, for example, in the opening sentence 40-4, which contains no fewer than five clauses:

[Now	40

it seems [that global warming is recreating the very

same conditions [which caused it [to stall before]]],

with the potential [to plunge the whole of northern

Europe into another Ice Age]].

Past examination questions also suggest that the examiners are interested in the relationship of clause structure to punctuation – close readers should ask how writers use dashes and semi-colons. The following extract from *The Economist,* taken from the 2006 'Higher' paper, illustrates this point:

> There is no doubt that obesity is the   35
> world's biggest public-health issue
> today *– the main cause of heart disease,*
> *which kills more people these days than*
> *AIDS, malaria, war; the principal risk*
> *factor in diabetes; heavily implicated in*   40
> *cancer and other diseases.* Since the
> World Health Organisation labelled
> obesity an epidemic in 2000, reports on
> its fearful consequences have come thick
> and fast.

A dash is often used to introduce a reformulation and elaboration of the earlier part of a sentence. Here the first sentence has the structure *There is no doubt that X is Y,* and the dash introduces three reformulations and elaborations of *Y.* The three reformulations are two highly modified noun phrases and one highly modified adjective phrase, all of which are separated by semi-colons. The 'pocket answers' to the Close Reading questions for this examination suggest that the 'semi-colons [are] used to separate items in a list which emphasises the serious/life-threatening consequences of obesity'. Teachers and pupils may be forgiven for considering this observation unhelpful. After all, any observation that the grammatical structure 'emphasises' the content is in danger of seeming trite. It is more useful to consider why the author felt the need to elaborate on the claim that 'obesity is the world's biggest public-health issue today'. The strength of this claim may incline some readers to consider it to be an exaggeration, and so the reformulations introduced by the dash provide three powerful justifications that support the initial proposition. Each of the three reformulations is detailed and complex, and so each is separated by a semi-colon to promote ease of reading.

The interplay between punctuation and grammar in any text is complicated and fascinating. Punctuation patterns change over time, and according to genre. Those texts designed to be read aloud may use commas and dashes to indicate pauses of varying length in oral performance. Literary texts that aim to represent streams of consciousness may use dashes to separate individual impressions or stray thoughts. Those texts that are designed primarily to be read may use punctuation to separate units of information. Any commentary on punctuation made by a close reader should take into account when the text was written, whether or not it was written for oral performance, the type of text it is, and how the punctuation interacts with the grammatical structure to aid the reader's comprehension.

10.4 Paying Attention to Discourse

The SQA 'Higher' questions are concerned not only with word choice and sentence structure, but the general impact of grammatical patterning as a stylistic feature and as a means of structuring discourse. This concern manifests itself in an awareness of repetition and variation, that is:

- repetition of grammatical features (lists of nouns, parallel clauses) for rhetorical effect; the cumulative power of lists (especially lists of three things)
- the way any variation to these parallel structures sets up a climax or contrast.

Lists pepper the SQA 'Higher' texts. The 'pocket answers' suggest that close readers are expected to identify and comment on some aspect of such lists. A typical example is an extract from *Time* in the 2003 specimen paper:

> Deluges, droughts, fires, landslides, avalanches, 1
> gales, tornadoes; is it just our imagination, or is
> Europe's weather getting worse?

The question in the Close Reading section of the paper asks candidates to identify one language feature that makes the opening sentence of this text 'dramatic'. The 'pocket answers' suggest that the examiners might be satisfied simply by the identification of the list of natural disasters, or the alliteration on *deluges/droughts* and *weather/worse* that characterises the two halves of the sentence. A perceptive close reader might go further and note that before the semi-colon the first half of the sentence is simply a verb-less series of nouns, while after the semi-colon there is a rhetorical question. The structure of the sentence therefore lays before the reader an extended series of natural catastrophes as the basis for an urgent question that involves both author and reader ('is it just *our* imagination').

The texts chosen for the SQA 'Higher' examinations are also characterised by a high degree of grammatical parallelism. Parallelism involves the repetition, usually with some variation, of a grammatical structure. We have already seen examples of this above, and one illustration, written by Ruth Wishart, is shown again below:

> Yet Ireland has managed to attract its young
> entrepreneurs back to help drive a burgeoning
> economy. *We must* try to do likewise. *We need*
> immigrants. *We cannot* grow the necessary skills   105
> fast enough to fill the gap sites. *We need* people
> with energy and commitment and motivation,
> three characteristics commonly found among those
> whose circumstances prompt them to make huge
> sacrifices to find a new life.

Here the parallelism sets up a contrast between modal auxiliaries expressing necessity and inability (*We must...We cannot*) and main verbs expressing requirements (*We need... We need...*).

One feature of grammatical parallelism is that repeated structures often come in threes, reaching a climax in the third variation on the theme. The example from *The Economist* is a good example of this, since the pattern of three is then repeated and inverted:

> *When the world was a simpler place*, [1] the
> rich were fat, [2] the poor were thin, and
> [3] right-thinking people worried about
> how to feed the hungry. *Now, in much of*
> *the world*, [1A] the rich are thin, [2A] the poor are   5
> fat, and [3A] right-thinking people are
> worrying about obesity.

Close readers note the role grammatical patterning plays as a rhetorical strategy; that is, how it structures texts in a pleasing and persuasive fashion. But in order to be able to do this, close readers must be able to identify what these patterns are. And in order to get credit for identifying these patterns, close readers must be able to describe them in accurate, technical language.

10.5   Conclusion

The preceding sections give an admittedly partial snapshot of the way that the SQA examinations in English have sought to assess candidates' grammatical knowledge. The questions currently included in the 'Close Reading' section of the SQA 'Higher' examination are certainly wide in coverage. The few examples given above range from commentaries on verb tense and modality to the length and structure of complex clauses. In other words, candidates are expected to be familiar with practically everything in this book and to be able to call upon that knowledge, if only for the sake of a handful of marks in one section of an extensive examination. Given that much time is required to acquire this facility, the pragmatic teacher and pupil might opt to sacrifice the paltry credit awarded for the acquisition of grammatical skill, and concentrate instead on the development of other skills that are more highly rewarded – for example, the skills of paraphrasing and summarising.

As we write, the 'Curriculum for Excellence' is being implemented and there is the perennial talk of redesigning 'Higher' English. We suggest that if curriculum designers truly wish attention to be paid to grammatical structure, they must reward the effort made in learning about it – and they may wish to decide which aspects of the many grammatical characteristics that *could* be learned about should be specifically targeted. Naturally, a common language of description needs to be disseminated amongst teachers. Some years ago, an electronic resource called *LILT* (Language into Languages Teaching) was developed by teachers of English and Modern Languages in Scotland, specifically with this aim in mind; it is available online at

http://www.arts.gla.ac.uk/SESLL/EngLang/LILT/frameset.htm

The language used to describe language in the *LILT* project largely accords with the descriptive framework used in this book. There are some differences, particularly because different languages are differently organised, and therefore sometimes require a slightly different terminology. Terminological quibbles aside, it is surely not beyond the capacity or the wit of today's educationalists to provide a systematic means of describing, teaching and assessing a core set of grammatical features. The increasing accessibility of free, online corpora with search tools means that rich resources are available for evidence-based grammatical analysis of speech and writing. (Further information on these resources is given in Anderson and Corbett, 2009.) Given the unarguable complexity of grammatical knowledge, teachers may reasonably demand more specific guidance about expected coverage of core concepts in future examination Arrangements documents – not just at 'Higher' level. We hope that the current book will not only help teachers, pupils and students to understand grammar, but that it will also help them engage more confidently in future public debates on the teaching and learning of grammar in Scotland today.

Answers to Activities

The answers given here are sometimes very precise, and sometimes more generally suggestive, depending on the nature of the questions.

Chapter 1

1.4   Discussion Topics

The quotations (i)-(iv) in (a) all express prescriptive (and sometimes highly dubious) beliefs about English. The rules of grammar are sometimes seen as a metaphor for an ordered and orderly society; Norman Tebbit and John Rae confuse the two; John Simon reveals his own ignorance about how language variation works; Anthony Lejune betrays some common misconceptions about linguistic systems and logic. Myths and prejudices about language abound; the study of language can enlighten us about them.

1.6   SCOTS search

Team is one of a set of words known as *collective nouns,* that is the nouns refer to a group of individual people or things. They can therefore be thought of as singular (one team) or plural (team members). Their agreement with verbs consequently varies, although British English tends now to consider collective nouns as plural, particularly in speech, and American English continues to take the traditionalist line and consider them as singular.

Chapter 2

2.6   Thinking about Meaning, Form and Function
Activity 1   'Jabberwocky'

	slithy	*gimble*	*raths*	*outgrabe*
1.	happy	amble	owls	hooted
2.	lovely	jump	ferrets	squeaked
3.	sly	frolic	beetles	hunted
4.	slimy	splash	leaves	rustled
5.	ugly	play	flowers	blossomed

You will of course have different words in your lists, but it is also almost certain that *slithy* will be one of a group of adjectives, *gimble* and *outgrabe* will be among groups of verbs and *raths* will be one of a group of plural nouns. It is just possible, if you have decided that *raths* is the present tense of a verb, that *outgrabe* will be an adverb (*the mome raths outgrabe = the farmer works outside, etc.*); however, a present-tense conclusion to the verse would not be in keeping with the past tenses of the first three lines. Remember, making substitution lists like these can help you decide the part of speech of an unknown word (e.g. here *slithy* must an adjective, since it is only replaced by Aj's).

Activity 2

A literal word-for-word translation of the Portuguese is given below:

O **Talco Johnson's baby** é feito com o talco
The Talcum Johnson's baby is made with the talcum
da mais alta qualidade e pureza, que junto
of more high quality and purity, that together
com sua exclusiva fragrância, deixa a pele
with its exclusive fragrance, leaves the skin
suave, macia e perfumada, protegendo-a
smooth, soft and perfumed, protecting it
contra o atrito e umidade que podem causar
against the friction and dampness that can cause
assaduras e irritações.
sores and irritations.

(a) **Form:** Note that Portuguese nouns often end in <*-idade*> (*qualidade, umidade*) and that the form of the noun affects the form of the adjectives which modify it (*exclusiva fragrancia...pele suave,* etc). Like English, the plural of the noun is formed by adding <*-s*> (*assaduras, irritações*). Verbs often end in <*-o*> (*feito, protegendo*).

(b) **Function:** Note that the order of modifiers and headwords in Portuguese Noun Phrases is different from English: *Johnson's Baby Powder* corresponds to *Talco Johnson's Baby*. The rules governing the use of the determiner *o/a* (the) are different too: first, there are two forms, and secondly, the definite article is used in Portuguese when it would not be used in English.

(c) **Meanings:** Perhaps you were able to work out much of the meaning by using 'cognate' words – words that are shared by both languages, e.g. *qualidade, fragrância*. However, knowledge of the grammatical rules governing Portuguese is necessary to figure out how the words fit together to make sense.

Activity 3

In sentences 1, 2, 5 and 10, *fast* is an adverb, and can usually be replaced by another adverb, *quickly*. In sentences 3, 6, 8 and 9, *fast* is an adjective, and describes various things. It cannot always be replaced by *quick* – no-one, for example, talks about the *quick lane* of a motorway, though *fast* in *fast lane* corresponds to the adjective *slow* in *slow lane*. In sentence 4, *fast* is a noun, referring to an event in which people refrain from eating. In sentence 7, *fast* is again an adverb, this time intensifying the adjective and meaning something like *totally* or *completely*.

Chapter 3

3.3.1   Exploring Open Word Classes

Activities 1-4 have no set answers since your individual searches will come up with individual results. They are designed to raise your awareness of the four main open word classes, and to familiarise you further with SCOTS searches.

Activity 5   Multiple Membership
Which word-class does *round* belong to in the following sentences?

a.	She had *round* blue eyes.	Aj
b.	Do you fancy a *round* of golf?	N
c.	The bus *rounded* the corner.	V
d.	Most soup-plates are *round*.	Aj

3.3.2   Texts A and B

Text A

1.	Av	7. pr
2.	N	8. a
3.	i	9. V
4.	d	10. n
5.	c	11. pn
6.	Aj	

Text B

1.	Av	7. c
2.	pr	8. d
3.	Aj	9. V
4.	pn	10. a
5.	N	11. i
6.	n	

Chapter 4

4.5 Activity 1
Label the *open-class* parts of speech in the following passage from Sheila
Mackay's *Mountain Music,* an extract from which can be found in the
SCOTS corpus. Think about the reasons behind your decisions – i.e. are you
relying on meaning, form or function, or a combination of the three? For
convenience, sections of the passage are numbered.

(1)   We **blethered** in **French**, our **only common language**.
             V   N   Av   Aj   N

(2)   He **spoke** of an **arduous journey**, many **months long**, over **deserts,**
            V   Aj   N   N   Aj   N
    dusty roads and the **sea** itself,
    Aj   N   N

(3)   to **get** to **Palma** where he **lives now** in a **barrio** with other **Sengali**
       V   N   V Av   N   Aj
    men.
    N

(4)   **Later,** I **bought UV sunglasses** from an **older man**
     Av   V   Aj   N   Aj   N

(5)   who **told** me he **had** a **wife** and several **children back home**
        V   V   N   N   Av Av

(6)   and that it would be one **year** and one **month** before he could **go back.**
                         N   N   V Av

(7)   He was **counting** the **days.**
            V   N

Notes: in (1) *French* could be classified according to its *form* as an adjective
(like *Sengali*); it has been classified here according to its *function* as the
headword in a prepositional phrase, a position normally occupied by a noun.
In (4) UV (ultra-violet) has been considered a version of the colour adjective
violet. It could alternatively be considered an abbreviation of a material that
restricts the passage of ultra-violet radiation, and so could be considered a
noun modifier. In (5) *had* is considered an open-class word because it is the
headword of a verb phrase; if the phrase had been *had got* then *had* would be
an auxiliary verb and so classified, in this case, as a closed-class item.

Look at the closed-class words in the passage. What can you say about their
role in the text compared to the open-class items?

Answer: Their function is largely to modify open-class items, or, in the case of the many pronouns, to prevent repetition. In comparison with the open-class items, they carry little meaning on their own. Try reading the text using the open-class items only. Then do it again with the closed-class words only.

Activity 2
From the <u>underlined</u> words in the passage, select examples of the following:
(a) a count noun **journey** **(b)** a gradable adjective **dusty** **(c)** a comparative adjective **older** **(d)** a non-gradable adjective **Sengali** **(e)** a possessive determiner **our** **(f)** an adverb of time **later** **(g)** a preposition **over** **(h)** a conjunction **and** **(i)** a main verb **blethered** **(j)** a modal auxiliary verb **would (k)** a pronoun **me**

Activity 3
You will have your own examples of this.

Activity 4
Label the underlined parts of speech in the following paragraph, also from Sheila Mackay's *Mountain Music*. Sort the items into open and closed parts of speech.

> At a <u>cornucopic</u> (Aj) vegetable stall, an ebullient young
> Mallorcan <u>offers</u> (V) me a Spanish lesson:
> '*Espinacas.*' Holding up a <u>bundle</u> (N) of dewy green leaves.
> '*Medio kilo, por favor.*'
> <u>Then</u> (Av) a bunch of plump green beans:
> '*Judias verdes,*' he smiles <u>as</u> (c) I repeat: 'Hoodias berdee'.
> The lesson continues, my basket fills, and <u>so</u> (Av) pleased is he
> <u>with</u> (pr) our joint effort that <u>he</u> (pn) throws in extra mandarins as
> <u>a</u> (d) reward.

Activity 5
Label ALL the parts of speech in the first sentence of the above extract by writing the abbreviation under each item.

At a cornucopic vegetable stall, an ebullient young Mallorcan offers me
pr d   Aj   N   N   d   Aj   Aj   N   V   pn

a Spanish lesson.
d   Aj   N

Note that *Mallorcan* has again been classified here as a Noun, according to its *function* (headword of a NP) and not its *form* as an Adjective. A case could be made for an alternative analysis.

Chapter 5

5.8 Activity 1

```
     M  M    H        H          x  M  H
(a)  (My entire being) (concentrated) (on the task.)
     NP d  Aj   N  VP    V        PP pr d  N


     x  M    H         H   H    H
(b)  (In my agitation,)  (I)  ( lost) (control.)
     PP pr d    N       NP pn VP V NP N


     M  H          H
(c)  (The car) (somersaulted.)
     NP d N  VP       V


     M  H      H    M  H
(d)  (The roof)  (hit)  (the rock.)
     NP d  N    VP V  NP d   N


       H       H     H
(e)  (Everything)  (went)  (black.)
     NP     pn     VP  V  AjP Aj


     M  H      H        H        x   H
(f)  (A nurse) (leaned)  (impatiently)  (over me.)
     NP d  N  VP V    AvP  Av      PP pr  pn


       H    H   x  H   x     H
(g)  (I)  (stared) (at her)  (in astonishment.)
     NP pn VP V  PP pr pn  PP pr     N


       M   H      H       M  H    H
(h)  (Dried blood) (coloured)  (my hair)  (red.)
     NP Aj    N  VP   V    NP d   N AjP Aj
```

178

```
      M  M          M        H     M  H     x  M  M    H
(i)   (A large yellow-blue-black bruise) (had spread) (over my right cheek)
      NP d   Aj          Aj         N  VP a   V   PP pr  d  Aj    N


        x     x   M  H
      and (round my  eye.)
        c      pr  d   N


      M      M   H     M   M   H    M   H
(j)   (That skeletal image) (might have been) (my reality.)
      NP    d    Aj  N   VP  a    a    V  NP d   N
```

Activity 2

Consider the sentences below. Imagine how you would explain to someone, using accurate grammatical terminology, why one sentence sounds perfectly acceptable, and the other does not:

> In *a very large whisky, large* is an adjective that describes the noun, *whisky*. It is a gradable adjective, and can itself be modified by the degree adverb *very* to signify, in this case, an increase in size.

> In *a malt whisky, malt* is a noun modifier that tells us the *type* of whisky it is. As a noun, it cannot usually be modified by degree adverbs like *very*.

How would you explain to a learner of English as a second language how the following phrases are constructed and what they mean?

Yes, I would say it's *very Perth* as well, to be skint

He doesn't seem *very rock and roll*, does he, Jasper Carrott

These are examples of the creative use of language to break the kinds of rule noted above with *very malt*. In other words, the degree adverb *very* seems here to be used to modify a noun. However, the meanings of the nouns here are actually more like adjectives – *Perth* means something like *Perth-like*, and *rock and roll* means something like *characteristic of rock and roll*. In other words, there would be a case, on the grounds of meaning and function, despite their form, for classifying these nouns as adjectives…in these unusual contexts.

Chapter 6

6.5   Activity 1   Phrases inside Phrases
From sentences 1-7 below, identify:

a)   one ambiguous Noun Phrase (7)

b)   two Noun Phrases containing an embedded Adjective Phrase (1, 6)

c)   two Noun Phrases containing an embedded Prepositional Phrase (2, 4)

d)   one Adjective Phrase containing an embedded Prepositional Phrase (5)

e)   one Noun Phrase with an embedded Genitive Phrase (3)

Activity 2
Once you have identified the phrase structures in Activity 1, analyse the whole phrase.

```
        M  M  M      H       H
1. (an    (extremely enjoyable) reading)
   NP d AjP Av        Aj        N


     M H   M x  M M  H
2. (a house   (with a stone stair))
   NP d  N  PP pr  d   N  N


     M M  H    H
3. (a   (doctor's) line)
   NP d  GP N     N


     M H  M x M  H
4. (a dog   (wi twa tails))
   NP d  N PP pr  d   N


   M    H  M x  M    H
5. (quite lucky  (with our neighbours))
   AjP Av   Aj PP pr  d    N
```

180

```
     M M M H   H
6. (a   (very good) job)
NP d AjP Av  Aj   N
```

```
     M     M    M  H
7. (more affordable rented homes)        or
NP  d       Aj     Aj   N
```

```
     M  M    H    M   H
7. (   (more affordable) rented homes)
NP AjP Av      Aj     Aj    N
```

Activity 3

Analyse the following phrases, extracted from the interview with Michael Stipe:

```
    M  M  H  M x M  M  M    H
1. (The lead singer (of the US stadium rockers))
NP  d   N   N  PP pr d  N    N    N
```

```
    M  M     H  M x M  H
2. (the biggest band  ( in the world))
NP  d  Aj   N  PP  pr d  N
```

```
   M H M x    M      H
3. ( a pair  ( of Woody Allen specs))
NP  d N PP pr     N       N
```

```
   M    M         H  M x H
4. (A <salt-and-pepper> carpet ( of stubble))
NP d  N    c    N      N   PP pr N
```

You can analyse *salt-and-pepper* as a single compound N if you wish.

```
   M  H M  x  M  H
5. (a quarter ( of a century))
NP d   N  PP  pr d  N
```

```
     M    H     M x M   M      H
6. (the figurehead ( of  a  global phenomenon))
NP d       N    PP pr  d   Aj      N


     M      M      H M x H
7. (an astonishing piece  (of music))
NP d        Aj        N PP pr N


   M H  M x  M       H
8. (a period  (of prolific writing))
NP d N  PP pr   Aj       N
```

Chapter 7

7.8   Activities

Try analysing these examples, taken from the children's story *Katie Morag and the Two Grandmothers* by Mairi Hedderwick (SCOTS Document 832):

```
        A M    M        M        H  S    H     P   H
1.      MCl [(One sunny Wednesday morning) (Mrs McColl) (woke)
        NP d    Aj        N        N  NP   N     VP  V


        O    H    A    H
        (Katie Morag) (early.)]
        NP    N    AvP  Av


          A H   P  H   S M  H
2.      MCl [ (Here) (comes) (the boat.)]
          AvP Av VP  V  NP d  N


          S       H        P H   A M   H   A x M  M H
3.      MCl [ (Granma Mainland) (lived)   (far away)  (in the big city.)]
             NP       N        VP V AvP Av  Av  PP pr d  Aj N


            x S  H   P H    A H   C M  M   M       H
4.      MCl [My, (you)  ('re)   (still)  (a smart wee Bobby Dazzler.)]
             i NP pn VP V AvP Av NP d   Aj  Aj        N


          S       H       P  H   O M  H    A  M   H
5.      MCl [ (Grannie Island) (revved) (the engine)  (very loudly.)]
             NP       N       VP V  NP d   N    AvP Av  Av
```

182

```
         S   H      P H  A  H
6.    MCl[ (Show Day) (was) (always)
         NP   N    VP V AvP  Av
```

```
      C  M  M  H   A x  M   H   M x  H
       ( a big event) (on the Island  (of Struay))].
      NP d Aj  N  PP pr d   N  PP pr  N
```

```
                         S M   H     A x M        H
There are alternative ways of parsing  (Show Day) and  (on the Island of Struay),
                         NP N   N     PP pr d        N
```

depending on the level of detail you want to give about the internal structure of proper nouns.

```
         S   H      P H  C  M       H      M  H
7.    MCl [ (Alecina) (was) (    (Grannie Island's) prize sheep.)]
         NP  N    VP V  NP GP      N        N  N
```

```
         x   S H   P H    A H
8.    MCl [ But  (all)  (ended)  ( well.)]
         c  NP pn  VP  V   AvP  Av
```

Chapter 8

8.6   **Activity**
a)   a complex sentence containing an embedded Prepositional Clause functioning as an Adverbial **(4)**
b)   a complex sentence containing an embedded Adverbial Clause introduced by a conjunction **(5)**
c)   a complex sentence containing an embedded Comparative Clause **(3)**
d)   a complex sentence containing an embedded Noun Clause **(1)**
e)   a complex sentence containing a Noun which is post-modified by a Relative Clause. **(2)**

Now try analysing the sentences fully.

```
               S   O H   S H  P H   P H C  M  M      H
1.    Se { MCl [ SCl [  (What) (you) (have)]  (is)  (an advance copy.)]}
               NCl  NP pn  NP pn VP V  VP V NP d  N      N
```

```
           A  H    P H   S M    H       M  S  H   P H
2.  Se{ MCl [ (Upstairs) (were) (loft bedrooms,  SCl [ (which) (had)
           AvP Av  VP V  NP V   N        RCl NP pn  VP V
```

```
    O   M      H
    (skylight windows.)])]}
    NP  N      N
```

```
           P H  S H  C  H   M x    H         M  x  S H  P H
3.  Se { MCl [ (Are) (you)  (happier  (in Morningside) SCl [ than (you) (were)
           VP V NP pn  AjP Aj  PP pr    N         CCl  c  NP pn VP V
```

```
    A  x  M      H
    ( at the Grassmarket?)])]}
    PP pr  d     N
```

```
           S...H  P M...S H   O  M  M   H      A   x  S H
4.  Se { MCl [ (We) (will (all) take)  (a keen interest) SCl [ in  (what)
           NP pn  VP a  pn V  NP d  Aj  N      ACl   pr NP pn
                    |_____|
```

```
    P  M  H
    (is happening.)]]}
    VP a  V
```

The above sentence includes a discontinuous element *we...all,* which together functions as the Subject. The discontinuity of the Subject is shown by the dots (S...S). *We all* has been analysed as a compound pronoun, the second part of which has been inserted (but not embedded) into the Predicator. Compare **We all** *will take a keen interest...*

```
           S M  H   PM  H   A x M    H      A    x
5.  Se { MCl [ (The bill)  (has moved)  (in that direction,) SCl [ although
           NP d  N  VP d   V   PP pr d    N      ACl   c
```

```
    S  x    P H S   H    M x  M     H
    (there)  (is)  (potential (for further reform))]]
             VP V NP  N   PP pr Aj    N
```

In this sentence, the ACl is an existential clause, with *there* as the dummy subject, and *potential for further reform* as the real Subject (See Chapter 7.2.1).

184

Chapter 9

9.12 Activities

Activity 1

1. modal auxiliary, third person singular, past simple subjunctive, intransitive.
2. main verb, third person singular, past simple indicative, intransitive.
3. main verb, third person singular, past simple indicative, intransitive.
4. primary auxiliary and main verb, second person singular (there is ellipsis of *you*), present simple imperative, negative, intransitive.
5. main verb, second person singular, present simple indicative, intransitive.
6. primary auxiliary and main verb, third person singular, present perfective indicative, transitive.
7. main verb, first person singular, present simple indicative, intransitive.
8. primary auxiliary and main verb, first person singular, present continuous indicative, intransitive.
9. main verb, second person singular, past simple indicative, intransitive.
10. primary auxiliary and main verb, first person plural, present continuous indicative, transitive.

All the verbs are in the active voice.

Activity 2

Make a complete form and function analysis of the sentences below. All contain different types of VP structure.

```
               S  H   PM  H      A  x   M    M      H
a.    Se { MCl [ (Jane)  (was talking)  (about her Wishaw childhood.)]}
               NP N  VP a   V     PP pr   d    N      N


               S M  M  H   P  H       O  M    M       H
b.    Se { MCl [ (A tall tree)  (twinkled)  (its Christmas message)
               NP d  Aj N  VP V      NP d    N        N

      A  x   M    H
      (over the statues.)]}
      PP pr  d    N
```

185

```
        A  H      S  H   P M  H    O H   Co M H
c.   Se { MCl [ (However,) (this) (has made ) (me)    (a sceptic.)]}
        AvP  Av    NP pn  VP a   V  NP pn NP d  N


         S M    M       H   M x  H
d.   Se {MCl [ (A concomitant impact  (on that))
        NP d     Aj      N   PP pr pn


     P M  H  O M H    M x  M       H
     (will be) ( a  switch  (to imported tobacco.))]}
     VP a  V  NP d  N    PP pr  Aj     N


         S  H   P M   M   M      H
e.   Se { MCl [  (They) (must have been delivered.)]}
            NP pn VP  a    a    a     V
```

Activity 3

1. The problem here is that present tense, perfective aspect *(have met)* is used in a sentence that specifies past time *(on Saturday)*. In such a context, either past tense, simple aspect *(met)* should be used, or the Adverbial should be changed to make the past time non-specific (e.g. *already*).

2. Here the problem is the opposite to that of (1). Past tense, simple aspect has been used with an Adverbial which expresses non-specific time in the past. However, note that this combination is permissible in American English. The British English equivalent would be something like *Have you seen her yet/already?*

3. Again the problem here is to do with aspect choice combined with the Adverbial. The Adverbial *(every morning)* expresses habitual action, not necessarily happening now. The progressive aspect expresses actions which have duration, and combined with present tense, this usually means that the action is happening now. With this Adverbial, the more acceptable verb form would be simple aspect, present tense: *He watches television every morning.*

4. Here the problem is the combination of Subject and Predicator. The Predicator has not been marked for agreement (concord) with the third-person singular Subject. It should be *My neighbour...plays...*

5. Here we have two clauses in a complex sentence, linked by a conjunction expressing simultaneity in time, *when*. The odd thing about the verbs in these clauses is that an action of long duration *(smoking)* is expressed as if it were a

186

single, complete action (past tense, simple aspect: *he smoked*) while an event of short duration (*I came in*) is expressed as if it had duration (past tense, progressive aspect: *I was coming in*). We would expect the aspects to be reversed: *He was smoking a cigarette when I came in.*

Activity 4

Much could be said about these pairs of sentences. The following brief notes are simply for guidance.

1. & 2.
Futurity is expressed through present tense. The propositions are treated as facts, not predictions. Sentence (2) adds the idea of duration to the event.

3. & 4.
Alternative ways of expressing predictions. Difference in formality?

5. & 6.
Sentence (5) is ambiguous – does it express obligation or deduction? When you add the idea of duration in (6) the sense of obligation seems to be lost, and only the deductive meaning of 'must' is possible.

7. & 8.
Sentence (7) expresses permission: who would say this? – the controller? When you change 'can' to 'could' the sense of permission changes to possibility – sentence (8) expresses a hypothesis.

9. & 10.
(9) expresses a completed action in the past. (10) does so too, but uses the present perfective, which is against the rules of standard English.

Activities 5 & 6

No suggested answers are given here for these activities. They are for your consideration and discussion. Try looking up these topics in different grammar reference books, some of which are listed in the *Further Reading* that follows. How consistent are the explanations given?

Further Reading

This grammar book is written within the main British grammatical tradition, developed by Randolph Quirk and his associates at University College, London. The first five books on the list come directly from this tradition, and are listed in order of size, shortest to longest.

1. G. Leech, M. Deuchar & R. Hoogenraad (1982, 2nd edition 2005), *English Grammar for Today*, London: Macmillan. [The bracketing method used in this book served as a basis for the method used in the present book. *English Grammar for Today* might usefully be bought as a supplement if you want more detail about the approach.]

2. G. Leech & J. Svartvik (1975, 2nd edition 1994), *A Communicative Grammar of English*, London: Longman. [Most of this book is intended for people who have already studied grammar; there is a useful summary at the end.]

3. R. Quirk & S. Greenbaum (1973), *A University Grammar of English*, London: Longman. [A medium-sized reference grammar where you can read up specific points at greater length.]

4. R. Quirk, S. Greenbaum, G. Leech & J. Svartvik (1972), *A Grammar of Contemporary English*, London: Longman.

5. R. Quirk, S. Greenbaum, G. Leech & J. Svartvik (1985), *A Comprehensive Grammar of the English Language*, London: Longman.

Like more recent descriptive grammars, the present book makes use of corpus data, in particular the SCOTS corpus. A pioneering project in this regard is the 100-million word British National Corpus (http://corpus.byu.edu/bnc/), and an even more extensive resource is the Corpus of Contemporary American English (http://americancorpus.org). Useful corpus-informed grammars of English include:

6. Douglas Biber, Stig Johansson, Geoffrey Leech, Susan Conrad & Edward Finegan (1999), *Longman Grammar of Written and Spoken English,* London: Longman.

7. Mike McCarthy & Ronald Carter (2006), *The Cambridge Grammar of Written and Spoken English,* Cambridge: Cambridge University Press.

The use of digitised corpora in language study is becoming a discipline in its own right. Good introductory books on this subject include:

8. W. Anderson & J. Corbett (2009), *Exploring English with Online Corpora,* London: Palgrave Macmillan [Includes further activities that make use of the SCOTS corpus, alongside freely available online corpora of British and American English.]

9. J. Sinclair (1991), *Corpus, Concordance, Collocation,* Oxford: Oxford University Press

If you continue to yearn for an authoritative guide to English usage, something that will tell you what you should do, rather than something that seeks to describe your linguistic behaviour, then the following guide is up-to-date, sensible and useful:

10. Pam Peters (2004), *The Cambridge Guide to English Usage,* Cambridge: Cambridge University Press.

Numbers 3-7 listed above are large reference grammars. They answer most thorny questions, and can be consulted in many libraries. Shorter but useful introductory books, in alphabetical order, by author, are:

11. N.F. Blake (1988), *Traditional English Grammar and Beyond,* London: Macmillan.
12. R. Bolitho & B. Tomlinson (1981, 3rd edition 2005), *Discover English,* London: Macmillan.
13. N. Burton-Roberts (1986), *Analysing Sentences,* London: Longman.
14. D. Crystal (1988), *Rediscover Grammar,* London: Longman.
15. D. Freeborn (1987), *A Course Book in English Grammar,* London: Macmillan.
16. S. Greenbaum (1991), *An Introduction to English Grammar,* London: Longman.
17. J. Hurford (1994), *Grammar: A Student's Guide,* Cambridge: Cambridge University Press.
18. H. Jackson (1990), *Grammar and Meaning,* London: Longman.
19. F. R. Palmer (1971, 1984), *Grammar,* Harmondsworth: Penguin.
20. L. Thomas (1993), *Beginning Syntax,* Oxford: Blackwell.
21. L. Todd (1985), *English Grammar,* Harlow: Longman.
22. E. Woods (1995), *Introducing Grammar,* London: Penguin.

If you have been challenged and stimulated by this book, and want to delve further into grammatical theory and related issues, then the following books are recommended:

23. S. Eggins (1994), *An Introduction to Systemic Functional Linguistics,* London: Pinter. [A reasonably reader-friendly introduction to a grammatical theory associated with the linguist Michael Halliday. Grammatical form and function are sorted into systems of meaning in relation to social contexts.]

24. S. Pinker (1994), *The Language Instinct,* London: Penguin. [A broad survey of issues related to transformational-generative grammar. Grammar is seen not as a social construct but as the outcome of innate mental processes, a universal 'mentalese'.]

The grammar of English is, of course, subject to change. If you are interested in how grammar changes over time, the following books are useful:

25. J. Smith (1996), *An Historical Study of English*, London: Routledge. [Explains various social mechanisms of change in the pronunciation, vocabulary and grammar of English, from Geoffrey Chaucer to Linton Kwesi Johnson.]

26. C. Hough & J. Corbett (2006), *Beginning Old English,* London: Palgrave Macmillan. [This is a beginners' guide to the oldest forms of English, written with a view to getting you started reading and understanding Old English literature as quickly and easily as possible.]

As the SCOTS corpus develops, new descriptions of language in Scotland will appear. A recent example, which makes use of early data from the SCOTS project, is:

27. Bergs, Alexander (2005), *Modern Scots,* 2nd edition, Munich: Lincom Europa.

Finally, the source of texts used in Chapter 10 to illustrate grammatical knowledge as tested in the SQA 'Higher' examination is:

28. Scottish Qualifications Authority (2006), *Higher English: Official SQA Past Papers with Answers 2003-6,* Edinburgh: Leckie and Leckie [This series is updated annually. The 'Higher' examination is due for one of its periodic revisions; the current regulations are available in the Arrangements documents on the SQA website: http://www.sqa.org.uk/]

Dictionaries

You are strongly advised to invest in a good desk dictionary, such as Collins or Chambers or the Concise Oxford. Do what few people ever do: read the preface to your dictionary. Become a critical user, and notice how the dictionary works and what it does well or badly. Pay attention to the grammatical information given for each entry. A particularly interesting dictionary from a linguistic point of view is the *Collins English Dictionary*, 9th revised edition, London: Collins, 2007. For Scots, see the *Concise Scots Dictionary*, revised edition, Edinburgh: Edinburgh University Press, 1987.

Index

List of Abbreviations

Adjective   Aj
Adjective Phrase   AjP
Adverb   Av
Adverb Phrase   AvP
Adverbial   A
Adverbial Clause   ACl
auxiliary verb   a
Comparative Clause   CCl
Complement   C
conjunction   c
determiner   d
Direct Object   Od
Genitive Phrase   GP
Headword   H
Indirect Object   Oi
interjection   i
intransitive verb   intr
Main Clause   MCl
Modifier   M
negative   n
Noun   N
Noun Clause   NCl
Noun Phrase   NP
Object   O
Object Complement   Co
Predicator   P

preposition   pr
Prepositional Clause   PCl
Prepositional Phrase   PP
pronoun   pn
Relative Clause   RCl
Sentence   Se
SPOCA
Subject   S
Subject Complement   Cs
Subordinate Clause   SCl
transitive verb   tr
Verb   V
Verb Phrase   VP

Brackets

(Phrase)

[Clause]

{Sentence}